A
Scriptural Guide
to Mary

Father Herbert Burke

Queenship
PUBLISHING COMPANY
P.O. Box 220 • Goleta, CA 93116
(800) 647-9882 • (805) 692-0043 • Fax: (805) 967-5133
www.queenship.org

Written in Honor of Mary
Queen of Angels and Saints

Then he said to the disciple,
"Behold, your mother!" (Jn. 19:27)

Table of Contents

Introduction

"I will put enmity between you and the woman...Then the dragon was angry with the woman, and went off to make war on the rest of her offspring, on those who keep the commandments of God and bear testimony to Jesus." (Gen. 3:15, Rev. 12:17)

When will the world join with God the Father (Lk. 1:26-28), God the Son (Jn. 2:11), and God the Holy Spirit (Lk. 1:41, 42) in honoring Mary as the Spiritual Mother of the Saints (Jn. 19:26, 27) and the Queen of heaven and earth? (Rev. 21:1) When will all those who seek Christ also seek her prayers to help them find him and follow him? The role of Mary has often been misunderstood and confused by Catholics and Protestants alike. In her imitation of Christ she has become the "stone which the builders rejected" (Lk. 20:17). The builders of the Protestant Church rejected the prominent role of Mary in Christian spirituality that evolved over the years from the early church to the present. This Marian minimalism has influenced Catholics as well. It is a baffling thing to see Catholics and Protestants look at the scriptures and get two totally different views of the role of Mary in God's plan for our salvation. The goal of *A Scriptural Guide to Mary* is to open the reader's mind to understand her through her role as the New Eve, The Ark of the New Covenant, the Immaculate Heart pierced by the sword of sorrow (Lk. 2:35) at the foot of the cross, the Queen Mother, and the Woman Clothed with the Sun. These are just a few of the keys to the Role of Mary in scripture that will be explained in this book, and recognizing them makes all the difference. As it says in Luke: "Then he opened their minds to understand the scriptures." (Lk. 24:45)

Jesus told St. John, "Behold your Mother." (Jn. 19:27) If we seek to be beloved disciples like St. John, leaning on the Sacred Heart of Jesus as he gave himself at the Last supper as the Bread of Life, faithful at the foot of the cross, standing next to Mary, then let us take her into our home as he did. With Mary as part of our spiritual home Jesus will be present and honored properly.

As scripture says: "When Jesus saw his mother, and the disciple whom he loved standing near, he said to his mother, "Woman, behold, your son!" {27} Then he said to the disciple, "Behold, your mother!" And from that hour the disciple took her to his own home." (Jn. 19:26, 27)

"One of his disciples, whom Jesus loved, was lying close to the breast of Jesus; {24} so Simon Peter beckoned to him and said, 'Tell us who it is of whom he speaks.' {25} So lying thus, close to the breast of Jesus, he said to him, 'Lord, who is it?'" (Jn. 13:23-25)

Let us be beloved disciples who love the Lord, who are close to his Sacred Heart and his Immaculate Mother, let us pray the Rosary daily, and adore the Lord in the Holy Eucharist. It is my hope and prayer that those who read this book will recognize Mary more clearly as their mother, and honor her as God has called us to. Christ is the King of Kings, Mary is the Queen of Queens, she is the "mother of all the living," (Gen. 3:20) of all those alive in Christ. (Rev. 12:17) The Holy Spirit inspires her to perfect love of God which is to be recognized and honored by the mystical body of Christ, the church. As scripture says:

"And Mary said, 'My soul magnifies the Lord, ... For behold, henceforth all generations will call me blessed.'" (Lk. 1:46, 48)

Fr. Herbert Burke
August 22, 2011
The Feast of the Coronation of Mary

Chapter 1

Mary, the New Eve and the Immaculate Conception

"And a great sign appeared in heaven, a woman clothed with the sun, with the moon under her feet, and on her head a crown of twelve stars...." (Rev. 12:1)

"The Lord God said to the serpent,... I will put enmity between you and the woman...." (Gen. 3:14, 15)

The key to understanding the role of Mary in scripture is the concept of Mary as the New Eve, as the Ark of the New Covenant, and as the Queen Mother. Many Catholics and non-Catholics are often confused about how the role of Mary is found in the scriptures. This is written to answer that question by touching on certain key topics that relate to understanding Mary in scripture. I write here mainly of those things that deal with Typology. Typology is the study of persons, places, things, and events in the Old Testament that prefigure persons, places, things, and events in the New Testament. Jesus uses typology (Jn. 3:14) and so does scripture in many places. (1Cor. 15:45, 1Cor. 5:7) Typology opens up a wealth of understanding in scripture. This type of study is often neglected or downplayed at protestant schools because of all the Catholic implications for Mary, the Pope, and the Sacraments it contains. I once spoke to a professor at a University who had a Ph.D. in scripture from a protestant school. He had never even heard of typology! Typology is the key to understanding the role of Mary in scripture. Once the concept of Mary as the New Eve, the Ark of the New Covenant, and the Queen Mother, are understood from scripture using typology, then all the doctrines about Mary become

1

clear. This was the way the church Fathers understood Mary, and they were taught by the Apostles. The fresh and original understanding of Mary in the earliest generations was through typology. The church has never abandoned these concepts, but preserved and defended them through the centuries. The traditional Catholic doctrines such as the Immaculate Conception, Perpetual Virginity, Assumption, Queen of Heaven, and Spiritual Motherhood all begin to flow clearly from understanding the scriptural typology of Mary.

I assembled some basic beliefs about Mary into a sort of Marian Creed. It contains many of the themes we will explain in this book. I will list this at the beginning to give the reader a framework of the path of understanding Mary we will follow in this book:

The Marian Creed

As Catholics we believe:

Mary was created by the Father,
to be the Mother of his only beloved Son,
And She became the Mother of God.

The Early Church named Mary the New Eve,
She is the sinless perpetual virgin who never disobeyed him.

Mary is the avenger of Eve; her heel is on the serpent.

She is not deceived into sin; she is faithful forever.

Her faithfulness is the foundation of the Incarnation,
And the beginning of our redemption.

The revenge of Adam comes through Mary's Son,
Christ has slain the serpent from the cross.

We believe that by the merits of Jesus Christ, God has granted Mary a singular grace.

As Eve was created in grace without sin,
Mary too would be created in grace without sin.

Hail Mary full of grace, the Lord is with you forever.

She is full of grace forever,

She is the Immaculate Conception,
She is the one perfect disciple of Jesus.

Mary was conceived without sin,
And she conceived by the Holy Spirit.

She became the Ark of the New Covenant,
Through Mary the word became flesh and dwelt first in her among us.

She was the living Tabernacle,
God chose her to be the first home of the Sacred Body and Precious Blood of Jesus.

Mary is the Mother of my Lord and my God,
With the Father we honor her with these Sacred Words, delivered by the Archangel, the Word of God says:
"Hail Mary, full of Grace, and the Lord is with you."

With the Holy Spirit we honor her with his words sent through St. Elizabeth:
"Blessed are you among all women,
Blessed is the Fruit of your womb Jesus."

At Bethlehem Mary held the infant king in her arms with joy,
Now at Mount Calvary, she holds her crucified son with sorrow.

Simeon prophesied her Immaculate Heart would be pierced with a sword.

Our Heavenly Father and Our Mother of Sorrows,
Beheld their only beloved Son dying on the cross for the sins of the world.

At the foot of the cross, Her soul magnifies the Lord.

From the Christmas joy of Bethlehem, when the Son of God became the son of man, To the agony of Mount Calvary,
Where the savior of the world gave his life on the altar of the cross.

Her contemplation of the Passion was the most perfect of all his disciples,
On Good Friday Her Immaculate Heart was pierced with a sword of sorrows,
On Easter Sunday She was consoled with joy at His Resurrection.

Christ ascended into heaven to the right hand of the Father,
He then called his mother to be at his right hand in heaven,
We celebrate her Assumption into heaven, body and soul.

She is a great Sign in the heavens,
She is a Woman clothed with the Sun,
She is crowned with Twelve Stars by her son,
She is seated at the right hand of her Son in glory,
She is the Queen of Heaven and earth,
The moon is at her feet.

The King of Kings has made her the Queen of Queens,
The Queen of Angels, and the Queen of the Saints.

She is the Queen Mother of the Son of David in the Eternal Jerusalem.

We honor her as our spiritual Mother in the Family of God.

She intercedes with her Son and joins her prayers to ours,
She joins her requests to mine,
From heaven she asks for our water to turn to wine,
Jesus says to us, "Behold your mother" and we honor her and ask for her prayers,
To his Queen he says, "Behold your son."

She is Our Lady of the Rosary,
She prays for us, she prays with us,
And she stays with us as our Loving Mother.

Through our faith and the Sacraments,
The Son of God dwells within us.

One with the Son, we enter into the family of God,
And Mary becomes our spiritual Mother.
He tells us from the cross, "Behold, your mother."

We honor her with the words of the Holy Spirit sent through his Holy Catholic Church,
Holy Mary Mother of God,
Pray for us sinners,
Now and at the hour of our death.

Mary is our Spiritual Mother, who loves us,
Who prays for us, prays with us, and stays with us.

Mary be at my side, at the hour of my death,
And lead me to the feet of Jesus,
That were pierced for the love of me. Amen.

The Little Marian Creed

As Catholics we believe:

Jesus Christ is the only beloved son of God the Father.

And the only beloved son of the Blessed Virgin Mary.

Mary conceived her Son by the power of Holy Spirit.

Mary is the Mother of God.

Mary is the New Eve.

Mary is conceived without sin.

Mary is the Immaculate Conception.

Mary is full of grace forever.

Mary is blessed among all women.

Mary is the Ark of the New Covenant.

Mary watched her Son die at the foot of the cross.

Mary's Immaculate Heart was pierced with a sword of sorrow.

Mary was assumed into heaven.

Mary is the woman clothed with the Sun.

Mary is crowned by her Son with Twelve Stars in heaven.

Mary is the Queen Mother seated at the right hand of her Son in glory.

Mary is the Queen of Angels and Saints.

Mary is our Spiritual Mother.

We honor her on earth.

She prays for us in heaven.

There are many titles given to Mary, and many artistic renderings of the various titles. Each title of Mary teaches us another aspect of her service to Christ. In Mark 6:3 Jesus is called "The carpenter, the Son of Mary." Pope Paul VI said at Vatican II quoting St. Thomas Aquinas: "As she gave birth to the head of the Mystical Body [Christ], she also gave birth to its members." The scriptures give us some of the basic titles of Mary. Speaking of Mary the scripture says:

Mary is "the Mother of Jesus." (Acts 1:14)

There are many titles given to Mary in tradition. Each title teaches us something about her, her relationship to Christ, and her relationship to the angels and the saints. Here are some of the titles she is given by tradition:

Queen of Angels and Saints—The Feast of the Coronation of Mary is Aug. 22.

Queen of Peace—Note that Christ is called Prince of Peace in Isaiah 9:5.

Our Lady of Grace

Mother of Mercy

Refuge of sinners

Mother of Good Counsel

Our Lady of Perpetual Help—June 27

Our Lady of the Rosary—Feast October 7

Our Lady of Mt. Carmel—Feast July 16

Our Lady of Sorrows

Our Lady of Victory—Tradition

Our Lady of the Miraculous Medal

Our Lady of Lourdes—Feast February 11

Our Lady of Fatima—Feast May 13

Our Lady Seat of Wisdom

Our Lady Star of the Sea

Our Lady Help of Christians

These titles given to Mary in scripture and in tradition help us understand who Mary is and how she can help us in God's plan for our salvation.

As we look at the various titles given to Mary in the scripture we see Mary is called "Blessed" (Lk.1:42, 48), "Virgin" (Mt. 1:23), "the Mother of Jesus" (Acts 1:14), "the mother of my Lord" (Lk. 1:43), "a woman clothed with the sun, with the moon under her feet, and on her head a crown of twelve stars...." (Rev. 12:1)

The Bible calls Christ the New Adam. "For as in Adam all die, so in Christ all will be made to live." (1Cor. 15:22) The early Church Fathers called Mary the New Eve. (Gen. 3:15) They said: "Death came through Eve, life came through Mary." A fallen angel deceived Eve, a sinless virgin (Gen. 3:4); she disobeyed God and brought death to the world. A good angel gave truth to a sinless "virgin named Mary" (Lk. 1:27); she obeyed God and brought life to the world. God uses the same instruments the devil used for our fall as the instruments for our redemption: two sinless sons of God—Adam (Lk. 3:38) and Christ, two sinless virgins—Mary and Eve, two trees—the tree of knowledge and the cross, two angels—Devil and Gabriel. We find this title for Mary as the New Eve in the earliest writings of the Church Fathers. These men wrote with the teachings of the Apostles from men who were taught by the Apostles themselves. Let us see the wisdom of the students of the Apostles as they teach us about Mary. The following words are among the first words written about Mary after the scriptures. These are among the first words of Christian "Mariology"; which means the study of Mary.

In the early Church St. Justin Martyr (120-165 A.D.) wrote: "... and that He became man by the Virgin, in order that the disobedience which proceeded from the serpent might receive its destruction in the same manner in which it derived its origin. For Eve, who was a virgin and undefiled, having conceived the word of the serpent, brought forth disobedience and death. But the Virgin Mary received faith and joy, when the angel Gabriel announced the good tidings to her that the Spirit of the Lord would come upon her, and the power of the Highest would overshadow her: wherefore also the Holy Thing begotten of her is the Son of God; and she replied, 'Be it unto me according to your word.' Luke 1:38" (St. Justin Martyr "Dialogue with Trypho," chapter 100, Source. Translated by Marcus Dods and George Reith. From Ante-Nicene Fathers, Vol. 1. Edited by Alexander Roberts, James Donaldson, and A. Cleveland Coxe. (Buffalo, NY: Christian Literature Publishing Co., 1885.) Revised and edited for New Advent by Kevin Knight. <http://www.newadvent.org/fathers/01287.htm>.)

St. Irenaeus (120-200 A.D.) writes on Mary as the New Eve in his work, "Against Heresies":

"In accordance with this design, Mary the Virgin is found obedient, saying, 'Behold the handmaid of the Lord; be it unto me according to your word.' Lk. 1:38 But Eve was disobedient; for she did not obey when as yet she was a virgin. And even as she, having indeed a husband, Adam, but being nevertheless as yet a virgin (for in Paradise they were both naked, and were not ashamed, Genesis 2:25 inasmuch as they, having been created a short time previously, had no understanding of the procreation of children: for it was necessary that they should first come to adult age, and then multiply from that time onward), having become disobedient, was made the cause of death, both to herself and to the entire human race; so also did Mary, having a man betrothed [to her], and being nevertheless a virgin, by yielding obedience, become the cause of salvation, both to herself and the whole human race. And on this account does the law term a woman betrothed to a man, the wife of him who had betrothed her, although she was as yet a virgin; thus indicating the back-reference from Mary to Eve, because what is joined together could not otherwise be put asunder than by inversion of the process by which these bonds of union had arisen; so that the former ties be cancelled by the latter, that the latter may set the former again at liberty. And it has, in fact, happened that the first compact looses from the second tie, but that the second tie takes the position of the first which has been cancelled. For this reason did the Lord declare that the first should in truth be last, and the last first. Matthew 19:30, Matthew 20:16 And the prophet, too, indicates the same, saying, instead of fathers, children have been born unto you. For the Lord, having been born the First-begotten of the dead, Revelation 1:5 and receiving into His bosom the ancient fathers, has regenerated them into the life of God, He having been made Himself the beginning of those that live, as Adam became the beginning of those who die. 1 Corinthians 15:20-22 Wherefore also Luke, commencing the genealogy with the Lord, carried it back to Adam, indicating that it was He who regenerated them into the Gospel of life, and not they Him. And thus also it was that the knot of Eve's disobedience was loosed by the obedience of Mary. For what the virgin Eve had bound fast through unbelief, this did the virgin Mary set free through faith." (*Against Heresies* St. Irenaeus) > Book III, Chapter 22 Source. Translated by Alexander Roberts and William Rambaut. From Ante-Nicene Fathers, Vol. 1. Edited by Alexander Roberts, James Donaldson, and A. Cleveland Coxe. (Buffalo, NY: Christian Literature Publishing Co., 1885.) Revised and edited for New Advent by Kevin Knight. <http://www.newadvent.org/fathers/0103322.htm>)

In his work, *On the Flesh of Christ,* Tertullian (160-240A.D.) speaks of Mary as the New Eve:

"As, then, the first Adam is thus introduced to us, it is a just inference that the second Adam likewise, as the apostle has told us, was formed by God into a quickening spirit out of the ground—in other words, out of a flesh which was unstained as yet by any human generation. But that I may lose no opportunity of supporting my argument from the name of Adam, why is Christ called Adam by the apostle, unless it be that, as man, He was of that earthly origin? And even reason here maintains the same conclusion, because it was by just the contrary operation that God recovered His own image and likeness, of which He had been robbed by the devil. For it was while Eve was yet a virgin, that the ensnaring word had crept into her ear which was to build the edifice of death. Into a virgin's soul, in like manner, must be introduced that Word of God which was to raise the fabric of life; so that what had been reduced to ruin by this sex, might by the selfsame sex be recovered to salvation. As Eve had believed the serpent, so Mary believed the angel. The delinquency which the one occasioned by believing, the other by believing effaced. But (it will be said) Eve did not at the devil's word conceive in her womb. Well, she at all events conceived; for the devil's word afterwards became as seed to her that she should conceive as an outcast, and bring forth in sorrow. Indeed she gave birth to a fratricidal devil (Cain, Gen.4); while Mary, on the contrary, bore one who was one day to secure salvation to Israel, His own brother after the flesh, and the murderer of Himself. God therefore sent down into the virgin's womb His Word, as the good Brother, who should blot out the memory of the evil brother. Hence it was necessary that Christ should come forth for the salvation of man, in that condition *of flesh* into which man had entered ever since his condemnation." (*On the Flesh of Christ* (Tertullian), Chapter 17. The Similarity of Circumstances Between the First and the Second Adam, as to the Derivation of Their Flesh. An Analogy Also Pleasantly Traced Between Eve and the Virgin Mary/ **Source.** Translated by Peter Holmes. From Ante-Nicene Fathers, Vol. 3. Edited by Alexander Roberts, James Donaldson, and A. Cleveland Coxe. (Buffalo, NY: Christian Literature Publishing Co., 1885.) Revised and edited for New Advent by Kevin Knight. <http://www.newadvent.org/fathers/0315.htm>.)

St. Jerome (331-420A.D.) summed it up by saying: "Death by Eve, life by Mary."

So, we see from these quotes that from the earliest times the comparison with Mary and Eve was there in the Christian faith. There is a balance of justice for us in that both genders of humanity share in the victory over sin. And, for God a balance is restored to his creation having a man and a woman without sin in the end of the world, as he did in the beginning of the world. So we see the Roman Catholic Church's Dogma of the Immaculate Conception of Mary, bound up with this early title of the New Eve. So, the victory of God and man over sin and the serpent is complete in the end, having used the evil of original sin to bring about the greater good of the redemption. The paradise gained in the New Eden is as superior to the one lost in the Old Eden as Christ the New Adam is superior to the Old Adam. As part of this plan of God the role and reward of the New Eve is superior to that of the Old Eve. So in the end God the creator looks forth to see the final formation of his creation vastly superior to the original creation which was marred by sin.

Sin becomes a temporary evil that leads the world to a greater eternal good. The role of Eve in the fall was not minor, and the role of Mary in the redemption was major. Those who seek to make Mary irrelevant to the redemption are blinded to the completeness and the beauty of God's plan for redemption. It is sad that the same serpent that deceived Eve now deceives many Christians about the role of Mary in modern times. The above quotes were some of the earliest written typologies of Mary; those who want to be like the early Church should look at their writings and see. To help understand the typology of Mary I developed this chart of parallels:

The Parallels of Eden and Calvary

The Garden of Eden	The Hill of Calvary
Adam,"Son of God" (Lk. 3:38)	Christ, "New Adam" (1Cor. 15:22)
Eve (2Cor. 11:3)	Mary (Lk. 1:27)
Eve: Created without sin	Mary: Conceived without sin
Death by Eve	Life through Mary
Mother of all living (Gen. 3:20)	Mother of all saved (Rev. 12:17)
Temptation by Lucifer, an evil angel to Eve, a sinless virgin.	Annunciation from the Good Angel Gabriel to Mary, a sinless virgin.
Eve disobeys God.	Mary obeys God.
Tree of Knowledge (Gen. 2:9)	Tree of the Cross (Jn. 19:17)

The Garden of Eden	**The Hill of Calvary**
Man and woman next to the tree at the sin (Jn. 19:26)	Man and woman next to the cross at the atonement for first sin (Gen. 3:6)
Forbidden to eat the fruit from the new tree of life (Gen. 3:22)	Christ gives us the Eucharist, from the tree of life the cross. (Mt. 26:26-29)
Punishment for the sin of Adam causes the ground to bring forth thorns. (Gen .3:18)	Bearing our punishment for sin, Christ is crowned with a crown of thorns. (Mt. 27:29)
Adam earned his earthly bread by the sweat of his brow (Gen. 3:19) in his labors on the cursed ground. (Gen. 3:17)	Christ earned for us the heavenly Bread (Jn. 6:51)of the Eucharist In the work of his passion, starting with sweating blood on the ground. (Lk. 22:44)
An angel is placed in the Garden to keep man out. (Gen. 3:24)	An angel is placed in the Garden to strengthen Christ. (Lk. 22:43)
The Side of Adam opened by God gives birth to his bride Eve during sleep. (Gen. 2:21	The Side of Christ, pierced by a lance gives birth to His bride the Church during sleep of death. (Jn. 19:34)
Exiled from Paradise. (Lk. 23:43)	Opened the gates of Paradise. (Gen. 3:23)
Driven from Garden. (Gen. 3:23)	Entered the Garden. (Jn. 18:1)
Clothed after sin. (Gen. 3:7, 21)	Stripped at crucifixion. (Mk.15:24)

Cain slays Abel. (Gen. 4:8)

The Good Thief (St.Dysmus) rebukes the Bad Thief. (Lk. 23:39-43)

Adam and Eve gave in to evil and brought death to all their descendants.

Christ and Mary overcame evil and brought life to all their spiritual descendants.

Warrior Women in the Old Testament Who Foreshadow Mary

"...where the Lord our God slew him by the hand of a woman." (Judith 13)

In the punishment to the serpent Gen.3:15, God prophesies that his head shall be crushed by the seed of the woman. The power of the serpent is in his head. Throughout the scriptures we see the servants of God, the seed of the woman, crushing the heads of the seed of the serpent—evil men who are symbols of Satan. The basic theme of Gen.3:15 is fulfilled in the Old Testament by both men (King David) and women (Jael, Judith). Then it is fulfilled in the New Testament by Mary and by Christ. Just as a man and a woman took part in the fall so too does God use both a man and a woman in the redemption. Compare the following verses:

"I will put enmity between you and *the woman*, between your seed and *her seed*..." (Gen. 3:15)

"And the dragon was angered at *the woman*, and went away to wage war with the rest of *her seed*..." (Rev. 12:17)

It is most humiliating for Satan when God uses a woman to be the instrument of His defeat. For this reason has God chosen the Blessed Virgin to be such a great assistance in His plan of salvation, just as the devil used Eve to be such a great assistance in his plan of damnation.

In the book of Judges we see Jael, a woman, defeats Sisera, the general of the Cananite Army. Jael is a symbol of Mary who defeats the serpent by her Immaculate Conception and obedience to God. Sisera is a symbol of satan since he is the head of the evil army attacking God's people Israel. She fulfills Gen. 3:15 by "crushing" his head. Scripture says:

"The Lord will have Sisera fall into *the power of a woman*...Sisera, in the meantime, had fled on foot to the tent of Jael...Jael, wife of Heber, got a tent peg and took a mallet in her hand. While Sisera was sound asleep, she stealthily approached him and drove the peg through *his temple* down into the ground, so that he perished in death." (Judges 4:9, 17, 21)

"Blessed among women be Jael...She hammered Sisera, *crushed his head.*" (Judges 5:24, 26).

Note how the word of God parallels Jael with Mary in Judges 5:24 and Luke 1:28, 42 where both are called, "Blessed among women."

Abimelech is a symbol of satan, and his skull is crushed by a woman. Scripture says:

"But a certain woman cast the upper part of a millstone down on Abimelech's head and it *fractured his skull*...Thus did God requite the evil Abimelech had done to his father." (Judges 9:53)

Another woman warrior of the Old Testatment is Judith who is a symbol of Mary, and Holofernes is a symbol of Satan. It is by the humble prayers of Judith (Judith 9:16) that Holofernes is defeated, so too it is by the humble intercession of Mary for us that God uses to defeat Satan's influence in our lives. Scripture says:

"Now therefore pray for us, for you are a holy woman, and one fearing God...falling down prostrate before the Lord, she cried to the Lord, saying: 'O Lord God of my father...Bring to pass, O Lord, that his pride may be cut off with his own sword. Let him be caught in the net of his own eyes in my regard, and do thou strike him by the graces of the words of my lips. Give me constancy in my mind that I may despise him; and fortitude, that I may overthrow him. For this will be a glorious monument for your name, when *he shall fall by the hand of a woman.* For your power, O Lord, is not in a multitude, nor is your pleasure in the strength of horses, nor from the beginning have the proud been acceptable to you; but the prayer of the humble and the meek has always pleased you.'" (Judith 8:29, 9:1, 2, 12-16)

Holofernes is the commander of the Assyrian army which is attacking Israel. Judith is a beautiful and holy Israelite woman who uses her beauty to trick the Assyrian Army and Commander into trusting her. Eventually he falls asleep drunk in his room alone with her. Scripture says:

"And Judith was alone in the chamber. But Holoferenes lay on his bed fast asleep, being exceedingly drunk...And Judith stood before the bed praying with tears, saying: 'Strengthen me, O Lord God of Israel...' And when she had said this, she went to the pillar that was at his bed's head, and loosed his sword that hung tied upon it. And when she had drawn it out, she took him by the hair of his head...And she struck twice upon his neck, and *cut off his head*... Then she brought forth the *head* of Holofernes and showed it to them saying: 'Behold the head of Holofernes the general of the army of the Assyrians; and behold his canopy, wherein he lay in his drunkenness, where *the Lord our God slew him by the hand of a woman....*' And they all adored the Lord, and said to her: 'The Lord has blessed you by his power because *by you he has brought our enemies to naught.*' And Ozias the prince of the people of Israel, said to her: '*Blessed are you*, O daughter, by the Lord the most high God, *above all women* upon the earth. Blessed be the Lord who made heaven and earth, who has directed you to the *cutting off the head* of the prince of our enemies, because he has so magnified your name this day, that your praise shall not depart out of the mouth of men who shall be mindful of the power of the Lord forever; for you have not preferred your own life' ...all blessed her with one voice, saying: 'You are the glory of Jerusalem, you are the joy of Israel, you are the honor of our people.'" (Judith 13:2-8,15-20, 15:9).

It is the "prince of the people of Israel," a symbol of Christ, who pronounces Judith, "Blessed among women" showing her to be like Mary. We see titles are given to Judith (13:20, 15:9), just as they are to Mary, yet it does not take away honor from God. God is pleased when we honor his faithful daughters, as a father is pleased when someone compliments his child. The father is pleased because it reflects on him, when his children are honored it proclaims that he is a good father and has done his job well. Judith like Mary is called, "blessed among women" (Judith 13:18, Lk.1:42). And Mary defeats Satan, as Judith defeated Holofernes, by her humble prayer and obedience to God. Judith (Judith 13:13, 15) and David (1Sam. 17:54, 57) carry the head of the enemy into Jerusalem and present it to the King. Thus, God uses both a man and a woman, to bring victory over his enemies.

David, who is a type of Christ, was a shepherd and King of Israel. He defeats Goliath, who is a type of satan. Goliath is a giant of evil, yet he is defeated by David. Scripture says:

"I will slay you and *cut off your head*... And he put his hand into his bag, and took a stone, and cast it with the sling, and struck the Philistine in the *forehead*. And the stone was fixed in his *forehead*, and he fell on his face upon the earth... And as David had no sword in his hand, he ran, and stood over the Philistine, and took his sword, and drew it out of the sheath, and slew him, and *cut off his head*... And David took *the head* of the Philistine and brought it to Jerusalem...And when David had returned... Abner took him, and brought him in before Saul, with *the head* of the Philistine in his hand."
(1Sam. 17:46, 49, 51, 54, 57)

Psalm 110 speaks of Christ:

"The Lord said to my Lord: 'Sit at my right hand till I make your enemies your footstool.' The Lord is at your right hand; he will *crush kings* on the day of his wrath. He will do judgment on the nations, heaping up corpses; *he will crush heads* over the wide earth."
(Ps. 110:1, 5, 6)

"And they came to the place called Golgotha, that is, the *Place of the Skull.*" (Mt. 27:33)

This is a symbol of the *skull or head* of the serpent. By his sacrifice on the cross Christ crushed the serpent's power, the venom of sin, the bite of death to the human race, while the serpent struck at his heel, and caused his temporary death.

"The woman said, 'The serpent beguiled me, and I ate.' {14} The Lord God said to the serpent, 'Because you have done this, cursed are you above all cattle, and above all wild animals; upon your belly you shall go, and dust you shall eat all the days of your life. {15} I will put enmity between you and the woman, and between your seed and her seed; **he shall bruise your head,** and you shall bruise his heel.'" (Gen. 3:13-15)

On the cross Christ defeats satan. Scripture says:

"Now is the judgment of this world, now shall the ruler of this world be cast out; {32} and I, when I am lifted up from the earth, will draw all men to myself." (Jn. 12:31)

"The reason the Son of God appeared was to destroy the works of the devil." (1Jn. 3:8)

The New Eve: Full of Grace; Empty of Sin (Understanding the Immaculate Conception)

"Hail, full of grace!" (Lk. 1:28)

Once we understand that Mary was the New Eve, it is easy to understand that she must also be a sinless virgin. Eve was the sinless virgin who brought sin and death, Mary was the sinless virgin who brought grace and life. Mary was prepared for this role by God, by saving her with the grace of Christ at the moment of her conception, rather than after. So, Christ is still her savior, but she is saved in a unique way to prepare her for her unique role as his mother. The Dogma of the Immaculate Conception:

"We declare, pronounce and define that the doctrine which holds that the Blessed Virgin Mary, at the first instant of her conception, by a singular privilege and grace of the Omnipotent God, in virtue of the merits of Jesus Christ, the Savior of mankind, was preserved immaculate from all stain of original sin, has been revealed by God, and therefore should firmly and constantly be believed by all the faithful."
—Pope Pius IX, *Ineffabilis Deus*, December 8, 1854

The Immaculate Conception means that Mary was conceived without sin. This was to prepare her for a special role as the Mother of God, when she would conceive by the Holy Spirit (Lk.1:26-38, Mt. 1:18, 19, 20). God chose to apply the anticipated merits of Jesus Christ to her soul at the moment of her conception and preserve her from original sin. The anticipated merits of Christ kept the good men of the

Old Testament, Moses, Elijah, etc. from the punishment of hell. They were prevented from going to hell in anticipation of the merits of Christ on the cross, and given a special place to stay. How did they merit this preservation from punishment if not in anticipation of the merits of Christ? For without the merits of Christ, they had sin which could not be forgiven. So, if God can apply the merits of Christ in such a way that he prevented Moses and Elijah from going to hell before Christ died on the cross, he can also apply the merits of Christ in such a way that he preserved his mother from sin at her conception. Where did the grace of God that forgave King David's adultery come from? Are only those born after Christ redeemed by Christ? Did someone other than Christ save the Old Testament saints? No, "there is no other name under heaven by which men can be saved." However, there are at times differences in the way some are saved by Christ. In scripture we see some have unique grace-filled events in their lives such as Enoch and Elijah (Gen. 5:24, 2K. 2:11, Heb.11:5, Mt. 17:3) and early resurrections. (Mt. 27:52-53) Seeing that God does unique things with his great prophets and holy men, how many more unique graces would he give to her who would conceive by the Holy Spirit—the mother of his only beloved son?! We should not try to limit God's power and means of salvation, especially when it comes to the Mother of God. Mary was saved in a unique way to prepare her for the fullness of her role as the New Eve and the Queen of Heaven.

In the beginning God created a sinless man and woman who fell. In the new beginning of redemption God would have another sinless man and woman who would never fall. There are only two people that the Gospels describe as "full of grace": Jesus and Mary.

"And he came to her and said, 'Hail, *full of grace,* the Lord is with you!'" (Lk. 1:28)

"And the Word became flesh and dwelt among us, *full of grace* and truth; we have beheld his glory, glory as of the only Son from the Father." (Jn. 1:14)

It is sometimes argued quoting St. Paul, "all have sinned" (Rom. 3:9-10), but he says this is for a general theological point. Romans make other general statements like all men receive the sin of Adam, and yet

18

we know that Jesus doesn't. We know that Adam and Eve were created without sin, and they had a special role together in the fall of man which brought sin. They were clearly different. If we understand that Jesus and Mary are clearly different because of the special role they have together in the redemption of the man, then it becomes clear. There are four people who began life without sin; Adam, Eve, Jesus (the New Adam) and Mary (The New Eve). To deny the victory of Mary over sin is to deny the fullness of God's victory over Satan through his creation of man and woman. If Mary is with sin, the victory over sin is incomplete. If Mary is with sin then the New Creation, the New Eden, is lacking balance. We must begin the new world with one man and one woman who have no sin. Otherwise God's victory is incomplete and he never restored what was robbed by the devil—one man and one woman without sin. So, as it was in the beginning before sin, God has restored through grace in the end. So as Christ was greater than Adam and was the source of grace for all men, so too Mary was greater than Eve and was an instrument of God's grace for all men. Christ corrects the damage of Adam; Mary corrects the damage of Eve. The Archetype of Manhood is found in Christ. The Archetype of Womanhood is found in Mary. As it was in the beginning, so it shall be in the end. A man and a woman serving God without sin means, creation is restored, creation is renewed, creation is redeemed. The Old Adam left the Garden of Eden and the Angel of the Lord guards the way to the tree of life and return to paradise. The New Adam enters the Garden of Gethsemane and leads us to the cross, the tree of life. From the cross he promises "paradise" to the good thief, and ultimately all of us repentant sinners. From the blood of the cross on earth we wash the robe of our soul clean of sin that we may go to the tree of Life in the new paradise of the New Adam:

"I am the Alpha and the Omega, the first and the last, the beginning and the end. {14} Blessed are those who wash their robes, that they may have the right to the tree of life and that they may enter the city by the gates." (Rev. 22:13, 14)

Chapter 2

Mary, the Ark of the Covenant

"Then God's temple in heaven was opened, and the ark of his covenant was seen within his temple; and there were flashes of lightning, voices, peals of thunder, an earthquake, and heavy hail. {1} And a great portent appeared in heaven, a woman clothed with the sun, with the moon under her feet, and on her head a crown of twelve stars." (Rev. 11:19, 12:1)

The parallels of Mary with the Ark of the Covenant go back to the scripture itself. The word of God clearly reveals the connection with Mary as the Ark of the New Covenant with the last verse of chapter 11 and the first verse of chapter 12. When John wrote this it was a continuous prose without chapter number interruption. Remember St. John didn't write in the verse numbers and chapters, we did. So the Church fathers naturally picked up on this theme of Mary as the Ark of the Covenant, and found more scriptural evidence in the study of typology. The Catechism calls her the Ark of the Covenant:

"Full of grace, the Lord is with thee." These two phrases of the angel's greeting shed light on one another. Mary is full of grace because the Lord is with her. The grace with which she is filled is the presence of Him who is the source of all grace. "Rejoice . . . O Daughter of Jerusalem . . . the Lord your God is in your midst." Mary, in whom the Lord himself has just made his dwelling, is the daughter of Zion in person, the *ark of the covenant*, the place where the glory of the Lord dwells. She is "the dwelling of God . . . with men." Full of grace, Mary is wholly given over to him who has come to dwell in her and whom she is about to give to the world." (CCC2676)

St. Ambrose (c. 339-397):

"The prophet David danced before the Ark. Now **what else should we say the Ark was but holy Mary?** The Ark bore within it the tables of the Testament, but Mary bore the Heir of the same Testament itself. The former contained in it the Law, the latter the Gospel. The one had the voice of God, the other His Word. The Ark, indeed, was radiant within and without with the glitter of gold, but holy Mary shone within and without with the splendor of virginity. The one was adorned with earthly gold, the other with heavenly." (*Serm.* xlii. 6, Int. Opp., S. Ambrosii) (*Blessed Virgin*, p. 77)

St. Hippolytus (c. 170-c. 236):

"At that time, the Savior coming from **the Virgin, the Ark, brought forth His own Body into the world from that Ark,** which was gilded with pure gold within by the Word, and without by the Holy Ghost; so that the truth was shown forth, and the Ark was manifested... And the Savior came into the world bearing the incorruptible Ark, that is to say His own body." (S. Hippolytus, *In Dan.*vi., Patr. Gr., Tom. 10, p. 648) (*Blessed Virgin*, p. 77)

Parallels of Mary and the Ark of the Covenant

"And the angel said to her, "The Holy Spirit will come upon you, and the power of the Most High will **overshadow you**..." (Lk. 1:35)

To help us understand Mary as the Ark of the Covenant, we need to look at the first major comparison is between Exodus 40:34-38 and Luke 1:35, and this shows God the Holy Spirit symbolized by a luminous cloud of glory. This cloud overshadows the Ark of the Covenant, and then this cloud overshadows Mary and she conceives by the Holy Spirit. This is when she becomes the dwelling place, the living tabernacle, the human tabernacle, the Ark of Flesh that contains the new covenant of the body and blood of Christ.

The ark was overshadowed by the glory cloud of God in Exodus, thus this cloud symbolizes the Holy Spirit. Interestingly the passage in Exodus helps us see the foreshadowing of the vigil light by the tabernacle in the Pillar of Fire by night and the cloud of incense used in Eucharistic Adoration which symbolizes the Glory Cloud of God seen by day. Scripture says:

"And he erected the court round the tabernacle and the altar, and set up the screen of the gate of the court. So Moses finished the work. {34} Then **the cloud covered the tent of meeting, and the glory of the Lord filled the tabernacle.** {35} And Moses was not able to enter the tent of meeting, because the cloud abode upon it, and the glory of the Lord filled the tabernacle. {36} Throughout all their journeys, whenever the cloud was taken up from over the tabernacle, the people of Israel would go onward; {37} but if the cloud was not taken up, then they did not go onward till the day that it was taken up. {38} For throughout all their journeys **the cloud of the Lord was upon the tabernacle by day, and fire was in it by night, in the sight of all the house of Israel.**" (Ex. 40:33-38)

We find the mention of the cloud symbolizing the Holy Spirit in the Transfiguration:

"He was still speaking, when lo, **a bright cloud overshadowed them**, and a voice from the cloud said, 'This is my beloved Son, with whom I am well pleased; listen to him.'" (Mt. 17:5)

And finally we find it in the Annunciation:

"And the angel said to her, 'The Holy Spirit will come upon you, and the power of the Most High **will overshadow you**.'" (Lk. 1:35)

The Catechism of the Catholic Church says:

"In the theophanies of the Old Testament, the cloud, now obscure, now luminous, reveals the living and saving God, while veiling the transcendence of his glory—with Moses on Mount Sinai, at the tent of meeting, and during the wandering in the desert, and with Solomon at the dedication of the temple. In the Holy Spirit, Christ fulfills these figures. The Spirit comes upon the Virgin Mary and "overshadows" her, so that she might conceive and give birth to Jesus. On the mountain of Transfiguration, the Spirit in the "cloud came and overshadowed" Jesus, Moses and Elijah, Peter, James and John, and "a voice came out of the cloud, saying, 'This is my Son, my Chosen; listen to him!' Finally, the cloud took Jesus out of the sight of the disciples on the day of his

Ascension and will reveal him as Son of man in glory on the day of his final coming. The glory of the Lord 'overshadowed' the ark and filled the tabernacle." (CCC 697)

The Second great parallel between 2Samuel 6:9 and Luke 1:43 is the similarity in the phrases used by David and Elizabeth. Both of them indicate a profound reverence and great humility in regard to the Ark and to Mary:

"And David was afraid of the Lord that day; and he said, 'How can the ark of the Lord come to me?'" (2Sam. 6:9)

The words of St. Elizabeth:

"And why is this granted me, that the mother of my Lord should come to me?" (Lk. 1:43)

The Third Great Parallel is between 2 Samuel 6:10-12 and Luke 1:56. It speaks of the three months of the Visitation of the Ark of the Covenant and of the three months of the Visitation of Mary. It is important also to note the similarity of locations where Mary and the Ark were outside of Jerusalem. The house of Obed-edom and the House of St. Elizabeth are both a few miles outside of Jerusalem! Scripture says:

"So David was not willing to take the ark of the Lord into the city of David; but David took it aside to the house of Obed-edom the Gittite. {11} And the ark of the Lord remained in the house of Obed-edom the Gittite **three months**; and the Lord blessed Obed-edom and all his household." {12} (2Sam. 6:10-12)

"And Mary remained with her about **three months**, and returned to her home." (Lk. 1:56)

Even the phrasing of the narratives begin in a similar manner:

"In those days **Mary arose and went** with haste into the hill country, to a city of Judah, {40} and she entered the house of Zechariah and greeted Elizabeth." (Lk. 1:40)

"And **David arose and went** with all the people who were with him from Baale-judah, to bring up from there the ark of God." (2Sam. 6:2)

The fourth great Parallel is between 2 Samuel 6:14 and Luke 1:41 where King David leaps before the Ark of the Covenant, and John the

Baptist leaps before Mary pregnant with Jesus:

"And David **danced** before the Lord with all his might; and David was girded with a linen ephod." (2Sam. 6:14)

"In those days Mary arose and went with haste into the hill country, to a city of Judah, {40} and she entered the house of Zechariah and greeted Elizabeth. {41} And when Elizabeth heard the greeting of Mary, the babe **leaped** in her womb; and Elizabeth was filled with the Holy Spirit {42} and she exclaimed with a loud cry, 'Blessed are you among women, and blessed is the fruit of your womb! {43} And why is this granted me, that the mother of my Lord should come to me? {44} For behold, when the voice of your greeting came to my ears, the babe in my womb leaped for joy.'" (Lk. 1:39-44)

In the Fifth Parallel we see the similarities between the contents of the Ark of the Covenant and Mary the Ark of the New Covenant. Regarding the Ark of the Old Covenant:

"For a tent was prepared, the outer one, in which were **the lampstand and the table and the bread of the Presence; it is called the Holy Place**. {3} Behind the second curtain stood a tent called the Holy of Holies, {4} having the golden altar of incense and the ark of the covenant covered on all sides with gold, which **contained a golden urn holding the manna, and Aaron's rod that budded, and the tables of the covenant**; {5} above it were the cherubim of glory overshadowing the mercy seat. Of these things we cannot now speak in detail." (Heb. 9:2-5)

Notice in the above quote the "lampstand" foreshadows the vigil light, and the "bread of presence" foreshadows the real presence of Christ, the bread of life, in the Eucharist. It is called the "holy place," and how much more holy is the tabernacle we now have in every Catholic Church that has Christ Himself in the Eucharist, the living bread of the real presence, which the old testament bread only symbolized! Although the author of Hebrews does not speak of these things in detail we will see some parallels between the Ark of the Old Covenant which prepared us for the Ark of the New Covenant here:

The Ark of the Old Covenant

1. It was made of wood and gold.

2. It contained the word of God in stone.

3. It contained the manna, the bread that fell from heaven.

4. It contained the Old Covenant the Law.

5. It had the Rod of Aaron, which symbolized the Old Covenant Levitical Priesthood.

The Ark of the New Covenant (Revelation 11:19, 12:1)

1. Made of the flesh and bones of Mary.

2. Contained the word of God in flesh; "And the word became flesh and dwelt among us..." (Jn. 1:14) "...we have seen with our own eyes..and touched with our hands concerning the word of life" (1Jn. 1:1) "that which is conceived in her is of the Holy Spirit." (Mt. 1:20)

3. Contained the living bread come down from heaven Our fathers ate the manna in the wilderness; as it is written, "He gave them bread from heaven to eat." {32} Jesus then said to them, "Truly, truly, I say to you, it was not Moses who gave you the bread from heaven; my Father gives you the true bread from heaven. {33} For the bread of God is that which comes down from heaven, and gives life to the world." {34} They said to him, "Lord, give us this bread always." {35} Jesus said to them, "I am the bread of life." (Jn. 6:32-52)

4. Contained the New Covenant in Body and Blood of Christ "This cup is the new covenant in my blood." (1Cor. 11:25) Contained the priesthood of the order of Melchizedek.

5. Contained the Body of Christ High Priest of the New Covenant: "where Jesus has gone as a forerunner on our behalf, having become a high priest for ever after the order of Melchizedek." (Heb. 6:20)

Note parallel: "Aaron's rod" (Heb. 9:4) "she brought forth a male child, one who is to rule all the nations with a rod of iron." (Rev. 12:5)

In the Sixth Parallel we see the connection between the Ark of the Covenant of the Woman in Revelation who is Mary and also symbolizes the Church. St. John first says that the Ark of the Covenant was "seen," next he says a woman clothed with the sun, and a crown of twelve stars "appeared." As the narrative continues there is no further mention of the Ark of the Covenant. We must remember that the numbers for chapters and verses were inserted later, but not in the original writing. So the narrative from chapter 11:19 to chapter 12:1 would have flowed without interruption. It seems as if this image was a prelude to the Woman who fulfilled what the Ark of the Old Covenant was only a symbol. Scripture says:

"Then God's temple in heaven was opened, and the ark of his covenant was seen within his temple; and there were flashes of lightning, voices, peals of thunder, an earthquake, and heavy hail. {1} And a great portent appeared in heaven, a woman clothed with the sun, with the moon under her feet, and on her head a crown of twelve stars." (Rev. 11:19, 12:1)

The Church fathers understood Mary as the Ark of the Covenant (Rev. 11:19, Rev. 12:1). Pope Pius XII wrote in *Munificentissimus Deus*:

"Just as the New Covenant surpasses the Old, so the new Ark of the Covenant (Our Lady) is superior to the old. The old Ark contained the word of God inscribed on stone tablets, but the new Ark contained the Incarnate Word of God. The old Ark held the Law that could not justify, but the new Ark held Jesus Christ Who Himself is the eternal New Covenant with God; He Who justifies and saves."

Chapter 3

Mary's Perpetual Virginity

"And Mary said to the angel, 'How shall this be, since I do not know man?'" (Lk. 1:34)

Why is Mary called a Perpetual Virgin? This is because she was a virgin, before, during, and after the birth of Christ. (Lk. 1:34, Is. 7:14) The Ark of the Old Covenant was a symbol for Mary the Ark of the New Covenant. Even this Ark was not to be touched by ordinary men:

"And when they came to the threshing floor of Nacon, Uzzah put out his hand to the ark of God and took hold of it, for the oxen stumbled. {7} And the anger of the Lord was kindled against Uzzah; and God smote him there because he put forth his hand to the ark; and he died there beside the ark of God." (2Sam. 6:6, 7)

The Second Vatican Council says:

"...at the birth of Our Lord, who did not diminish his mother's virginal integrity but sanctified it." (Vat.II LG57)

At Mass Catholics show their belief in Mary's perpetual virginity when they say, "Blessed Mary, Ever Virgin" in the Penitential Rite. The same divine power which intervened in Mary's life to allow her to conceive in a supernatural way preserved her virginity in conception and in birth, the virgin birth.

The statement by Mary in Luke makes much more sense, if we understand it in this way. A deeper understanding of Luke 1:34, "How can this be since I do not know man," points out that Mary said this, not because she was ignorant of the way sexual relations work, but because she had intended to remain a virgin even after marriage. This must be the case, otherwise she would have naturally assumed Joseph would be the Father, since she was already betrothed/engaged to him at the time. Thus, her question to the angel only makes sense if understood in this way. Tradition says that both Mary and Joseph had made special promises to God, to remain virgins. In light of the teachings of the Hebrew Community of the Essenes which valued abstinence even within marriage, this is not in conflict with Hebrew beliefs of the time. After becoming the Spouse of the Holy Spirit, and the Mother of God, it would not be fitting for her to then unite with a man and have children by someone else. The fact that Mary had no children is indicated by her care being given to a friend, not to a relative of Jesus. So at his death Jesus would not have entrusted the care of Mary to John if she had other sons besides Jesus to take care of her. (Jn. 19:26)

Scripture never mentions any other Son of Mary besides Jesus. Scripture makes no mention of "sons of Mary" (Mk. 6:3), but only "brothers of Jesus." In the Old Testament, the term brother is frequently used for a nephew or cousin (Gen. 13:8). The term "brother" in New Testament Greek was the rendition of the translators from the Hebrew word for "kinsman" to "brother." Even today among the semites the word "brother" would include cousins as well. The term "brothers" does not literally mean what the English translation implies since Semites use the same word for true blood relatives as they do for brothers.

The care of Mary was given over to a friend, not a relative of Jesus. (Jn. 19:26) This would not occur if Mary had other children to provide for her. The translation of the word "until," which occurs in some bibles in Matthew 1:25, does not necessarily imply a change afterwards, see (2Sam. 6:23). Matthew 1:18 asserts that there were no relations between Mary and Joseph before the conception of Jesus, to make it clear she conceived by the Holy Spirit. The passage does not imply anything considering that which came afterwards. The people thought Joseph was the Father of Jesus. (Mt. 13:55) Matthew 27:56 mentions "Mary, the mother of James and Joseph," who are the same relatives of Jesus that are mentioned in Matthew 13:55. Thus, it shows that their mother is not the same Mary who is the Mother of Jesus, as John 19:25 clearly shows. Some translations use the word "till" in Matthew 1:25 in reference to the Virgin Birth.

"And he did not know her till she brought forth her first born son." (Mt. 1:25)

Some have used this wording to argue against the perpetual virginity of Mary. If we study the use of the word "till" in Matthew 1:25 and compare it with Psalm 110:1— "Sit at my right hand, till I make your enemies your footstool"—we see that the word describes what happens up to, but not after. See also: 2Sam. 6:23, Gen. 8:7. Also, Matthew 1:25 speaks of the firstborn, but this does not mean that there was a secondborn. "Firstborn" is an honorary title from scripture that can be given to an only child. Scripture says:

"Consecrate to me every firstborn that opens the womb among the Israelites, both of man and beast, for it belongs to me." (Ex. 13:2)

The use of the term "bretheren" or "brothers of the Lord" (Mt. 12:46, Acts 1:14) does not necessarily mean an actual brother of Jesus the way we use the term in English. In Genesis14:14, Lot is called Abraham's brother, yet Genesis 11:27 describes his relationship to Lot, how he was his uncle. A similar example is found with Jacob who is called the "brother" of his uncle Laban. (Gen. 29:15) The original Greek word meant relatives, which could mean brothers or cousins. Scripture never makes reference to the children of Mary and Joseph. Also, Jesus entrusted the care of His mother to the Apostle John (Jn.19:27), indicating she had no other sons to take care of her after the death of Jesus.

Even the three main Protestant Reformers Luther, Calvin, and Zwingli, did not dispute Mary's Perpetual Virginity.

Zwingli: (Jan. 1528) I speak of this in the holy church of Zurich, and in all my writings I recognize Mary as ever virgin and holy.

Luther: A virgin before the conception and birth, she remained a virgin also at the birth, and after it.

Calvin: Commentary on Matthew 13:55: "We have already said in another place that according to the custom of the Hebrews all relatives were called 'bretheren.'" Commentary on Matthew1:25: "Concerning what has happened since this birth the writer of the gospel says nothing. Certainly it is a matter about which no one will cause dispute unless he is somewhat curious. On the contrary, there never was a man who would contradict this [perpetual virginity] in obstinancy unless he were a pigheaded and fatuous person."

There have been certain folk who have wished to suggest from this passage that the Virgin Mary had other children than the Son of God, and that Joseph had dwelt with her later, but what folly this is. For the gospel writer did not wish to record what happened afterwards he simply wished to make clear, Joseph's obedience and to show also that Joseph had been well and truly assured that it was God who sent his angel to Mary. He had therefore never dwelt with her, nor had he ever shared her company, and this besides our Lord is called the firstborn. This is not because there was a second or a third but because the gospel writer is paying regard to the precedence. Scripture speaks nothing of naming the firstborn whether or not there was any question of the second."

Chapter 4

Mary in the Apocalypse

"And a great sign appeared in heaven, a woman clothed with the sun, with the moon under her feet, and on her head a crown of twelve stars." (Rev. 12:1)

From the Cross to the Sun

God's love has brought Mary from a woman clothed with sorrow at the foot of the cross to a woman clothed with the Sun in glory! Who is the woman of Revelation 12:1? Does this woman represent Mary, the Church, or both? If we look at the various clues discussed over the centuries I believe we will find this woman is Mary, who is also a type or symbol of the Church, the New Israel. I find it amusing that so many modern non-Catholic commentaries on Revelation 12:1 start out by arguing, "This is not Mary!" If the modernist commentators have to work so hard to convince the reader it's not Mary, what was the original writer trying to show the reader? Perhaps the idea that the woman who gives birth to Jesus is not Mary presents a challenge to those who wish to argue against a Marian identity. The confusion arises from the fact that this chapter, like much of Revelation, is an interplay between time and eternity, the symbolic and the literal. If we consider the reality that Jesus goes on a mini-exodus "out of Egypt I have called my son" (Mt. 2:15) as interpreted by the Evangelist, things start to make more sense. After all, Mary was carrying Jesus in her arms when they fled to and from the desert of Egypt. So the mention of the waters and the earth swallowing them up tends to be some allusion to the time Israel crossed the sea on dry land. Alongside Jesus, Mary too is a glory of Israel. She is the Ark of the New Covenant and the Ark of the Covenant crossed on dry land through the river Jordan. The Eagle's wings enable her to fly away from the serpent. (Rev. 12:14) This could point out how her sinlessness brought her above the devil and the things of this world. We know she escapes the dragon and it sure makes him mad! (Rev. 12:15-17) How do we escape the devil, if not by avoiding sin. If we see how the life of Jesus as recorded here goes from the Nativity to the Ascension (Rev. 12:5), without mention of what was in between, we understand how the time flow of this chapter is not necessarily following the usual understanding. We may also notice that the mention of the Great War in heaven, which began before the creation, is mentioned next. (Rev. 12:7) So there is obviously a connection between the rebellion and punishment of Satan in heaven with the Woman and her Son in Revelation 12. What is the first thing that the dragon does when he is thrown down to the earth, he goes after the woman! (Rev. 12:13) Why would he go after her, to get her to sin! The polluted water of Satan's vomit (Rev. 12:15) is filled with temptations and sins. Scripture uses this term vomit to point to dirty waters of sin:

"For it would have been better for them never to have known the way of righteousness than after knowing it to turn back from the holy commandment delivered to them. {22} It has happened to them according to the true proverb, The dog turns back to his own vomit." (2Pt. 2:21, 22)

"But she escapes the dragon and sin. O Mary, Conceived without sin, pray for us who have recourse to thee! We need your prayers for the devil makes war on your offspring, those who keep the commandments of God and give witness to Jesus." (Rev. 12:17)

So, who is this woman in Revelation 12:1? We know she gives birth to Jesus described as a "child who will rule the nations with an iron rod," that would be the first big clue that it is Mary. As we look through the passage we find it filled with symbolism. It reads as a mystical or spiritual description of Mary, and a layered time compression series of events. There are some things in the passage which seem to be difficult to apply to Mary as an individual and point rather to her as a symbol of the Church. Mary is a type of the church because she is the fulfillment of what the church should be, she is the most faithful disciple of Jesus. So, it is important not to let references in the passage which come later overshadow the identity established at the beginning of the chapter when it speaks of her giving birth to Jesus. These references have caused some commentaries to see only ancient Israel, or the Church exclusively, and deny Mary's place completely in the identity of the woman in Revelation 12:1. So we will look at things which help us recognize Mary as the woman in Revelation 12. Pope Pius X writes in paragraph 24 of *Ad diem illum laetissimum*:

"{24} Leaving aside charity towards God, who can contemplate the Immaculate Virgin without feeling moved to fulfill that precept which Christ called peculiarly His own, namely that of loving one another as He loved us? "A great sign," thus the Apostle St. John describes a vision divinely sent him, appears in the heavens: "A woman clothed with the sun, and with the moon under her feet and a crown of twelve stars upon her head." (Apoc. xii., 1) **Everyone knows that this woman signified the Virgin Mary**, the stainless one who brought forth our Head. The Apostle continues: "And, being with child, she cried travailing in birth, and was in pain to be delivered." (Apoc. xii., 2) John therefore saw the Most Holy Mother of God already in eternal happiness, yet travailing in a mysterious childbirth. What birth was it? Surely it was the birth of us who, still in exile, are yet to be generated to the perfect charity of God, and to eternal happiness. And the birth pains show the love and desire with which the Virgin from heaven above watches over us, and strives with unwearying prayer to bring about the fulfillment of the number of the elect."

(Electronic Copyright © 1999 EWTN All Rights Reserved Provided Courtesy of: Eternal Word Television Network 5817 Old Leeds Road Irondale, AL 35210*www.ewtn.com*)

We see Micah talks about "travail" and Revelation 12:2 talks about "anguish":

"But you, O Bethlehem Ephrathah, who are little to be among the clans of Judah, from you shall come forth for me one who is to be ruler in Israel, whose origin is from of old, from ancient days. {3} Therefore he shall give them up until the time when she who is in travail has brought forth; then the rest of his brethren shall return to the people of Israel. {4} And he shall stand and feed his flock in the strength of the Lord, in the majesty of the name of the Lord his God. And they shall dwell secure, for now he shall be great to the ends of the earth." (Micah 5:2-4)

"She was with child and she cried out in her pangs of birth, in anguish for delivery." (Rev. 2:2)

"But standing by the cross of Jesus were his mother, and his mother's sister, Mary the wife of Clopas, and Mary Magdalene. {26} When Jesus saw his mother, and the disciple whom he loved standing near, he said to his mother, 'Woman, behold, your son!' {27} Then he said to the disciple, 'Behold, your mother!'" (Jn. 19:25-27)

The suffering of Jesus was also shared by his disciples who wept, but none as much as by the woman who bore him. Watching her son die on the cross is the moment of "travail" and "anguish" when Jesus informs Mary she will have his disciples as her new "children." Scripture says:

"Truly, truly, I say to you, you will weep and lament, but the world will rejoice; you will be sorrowful, but your sorrow will turn into joy. {21} **When a woman is in travail she has sorrow, because her hour has come;** but when she is delivered of the child, she no longer remembers the anguish, for joy that a child is born into the world. {22} So you have sorrow now, but I will see you again and your hearts will rejoice, and no one will take your joy from you." (Jn. 16:20-22)

If the suffering of the apostles at the loss of the Lord could be compared to a woman in giving birth, what were the sufferings of the Mother who did give birth to him being present at the foot of the cross? In a certain way, Jesus word's were more directly applicable to Mary. **When a woman is in travail she has sorrow, because her hour has come.** Mary's hour came with Jesus' hour, for they are linked together in a mystical union, "What would you have me do woman? My hour has not yet come." (Jn. 2:4) At the wedding of Cana her hour of request brought his hour of fulfillment. At the foot of the cross his hour of sacrifice brought her greatest hour of suffering. Her suffering at the foot of the cross was the greatest because her knowledge and love for Jesus was the greatest.

"And I will pour out on the house of David and the inhabitants of Jerusalem a spirit of compassion and supplication, so that, when they **look on him whom they have pierced, they shall mourn for him, as one mourns for an only child, and weep bitterly over him, as one weeps over a first-born.** (Zech. 12:10) [Mary is truly the "one who mourns" Zech. 12:10, for Jesus her only child.]

The *pietà* and the thirteenth station of the cross, show the sorrow and travail spoken of in Revelation 12:2 and the external view of the sorrowful scene where the Immaculate heart is pierced with a sword of sorrow as prophesied by Simeon. (Lk.2:35) From the cross to the sun Mary was the handmaid who would be Queen, the supreme Saint of Saints who reigns to serve. Suffering in silence her sacrifice was to watch the redemption of the world, and to feel it like no one else. Clothed in sorrow at the foot of the cross, she was destined by God to be clothed with the sun in heaven. The face filled with tears on earth would be crowned with stars in heaven. Her Immaculate heart was filled with sorrow at the death of her son because she who had no sin saw the effect of sin on her Son.

However there would be Joy because "when she is delivered of the child, she no longer remembers the anguish, for joy that a child is born into the world." (Jn. 16:21) Who is born of Mary at the foot of the cross? "He said to his mother, 'Woman, behold, your son!' {27} Then he said to the disciple, 'Behold, your mother!'" (Jn. 19:27) John was born, the firstborn of the cross. So, we begin to see the connection between the birth pangs and the cross, the birth of Christ and the birth of the mystical body of Christ, the Church. Mary gave birth to both. "She cried out in her pangs of birth, in anguish for delivery." (Rev. 12:2) And now we see who Mary's other children are: "Then the dragon was angry with the woman, and went off to make war on the rest of her offspring, on those who keep the commandments of God and bear testimony to Jesus." (Rev. 12:17)

The Church is the Family of God, and Mary is the Mother of God. She is the mother of the Church the Mother of the Family of God. The

Church is the body of Christ: "The Church which is his body." (Eph. 1:23) Mary gave birth to the body of Christ, both physical and mystical. She gave birth to the Christ who is the head, and to the church which is the body. "...for the church, {23} which is his body." (Eph. 1:23) The birth of the sinless Christ was with joy, but the birth of the sinful church was with much pain.

She gave birth to the body of Christ. His body came from her body. This is true physically for Christ and spiritually for the Church: His spiritual/mystical body. Mary's role in the church, the body of Christ, is to be the source and container of the body, hence she is the Ark of the New Covenant. Mary is the hinge of humanity through which Christ entered the family of man. Christ is the door through which man enters the family of God. In the plan of redemption her role is the Mother of the Church, as the most faithful disciple she is representatively a symbol for the church. If we look at the analogy St.Paul gives for members of the body of the Christ for the Church, and the different roles people have, what role do we imagine for Mary? What role does she have in the family of God? (Eph. 3:15) She is the mother of the Church:

"For just as the body is one and has many members, and all the members of the body, though many, are one body, so it is with Christ. {13} For by one Spirit we were all baptized into one body—Jews or Greeks, slaves or free—and all were made to drink of one Spirit. {14} For the body does not consist of one member but of many. {15} If the foot should say, 'Because I am not a hand, I do not belong to the body,' that would not make it any less a part of the body. {16} And if the ear should say, 'Because I am not an eye, I do not belong to the body,' that would not make it any less a part of the body. {17} If the whole body were an eye, where would be the hearing? If the whole body were an ear, where would be the sense of smell? {18} But as it is, God arranged the organs in the body, each one of them, as he chose. {19} If all were a single organ, where would the body be? {20} As it is, there are many parts, yet one body. {21} The eye cannot say to the hand, 'I have no need of you,' nor again the head to the feet, 'I have no need of you.' {22} On the contrary, the parts of the body which seem to be weaker are indispensable, {23} and those parts of the body which we think less honorable we invest with the greater honor, and our unpresentable parts are treated with greater modesty, {24} which our more presentable parts do not require. But God has so composed the body, giving the greater honor to the inferior part, {25} that there may be no discord in the body, but that the members may have the same care for one another. {26} If one member suffers, all suffer together; **if one member is honored, all rejoice together**. {27} Now you are the body of Christ and individually members of it.'" (1Cor. 12:12-27)

Mary is honored the most, as St. Paul says above: "if one member is honored, all rejoice together." (1Cor. 12:27) Christ is the head of the body; Mary is the Mother of the body of Christ. So Mary is our spiritual Mother, she is the New Eve, the mother of all those living in Christ: "...the dragon was angry with the woman, and went off to make war on the rest of her offspring, on those who keep the commandments of God and bear testimony to Jesus." (Rev. 12:17) The man called his wife's name Eve, because she was the mother of all living." (Gen. 3:20) Thus, Christ is the New Adam, Mary is the New Eve, and the Church is the family of God.

Those who argue against the identity of the Woman in Revelation 12 being Mary have some big questions to answer. The woman clearly gives birth to Jesus, if she isn't Mary who is she? If this woman is seen as the Church exclusively, then do they say the church gives birth to itself? Is that not strange, unnatural, illogical, and against the understanding of family given by God Himself? Are we not Sons of the Father when Christ dwells within us? Did not Mary conceive by the Holy Spirit? Did she not give birth to God the Son? Is she not the Mother of God? Is she not made by this role the mother of the children of God? Can she be the mother of Jesus and not be our mother? Can we be brothers of Jesus and have a different mother than Jesus? Can the Father of Jesus be our Father, and the Mother of Jesus not be our mother? Are we in the family of God, but lacking a mother? Does not the family of God have a mother? If the woman in Revelation 12 gives birth to Jesus, and her other children keep the commandments and give witness to Jesus, can she be someone besides Mary? If the woman in Revelation 12 is identified only as the church isn't there a big problem? Can the children be their own mother? No, I think the family of God, has a Mother, and her name is Mary. **The woman in Revelation 12 gives birth to Jesus, and the Church. She signifies the Church in her being, but in her person she is the mother in Revelation 12:1. She is Mary!**

If we look at the characters shown in Revelation 12 we find each one is a real individual person, and not some collective being. The Woman is Mary, the child is Jesus, the dragon is the devil, and the Archangel is Michael. To have three of these four major characters in the chapter be individuals, and one of them be exclusively a symbol of many people, is incongruous.

The Creation of the "Woman" in the Apocalypse

"Then the man said, 'This at last is bone of my bones and flesh of my flesh; she shall be called Woman, because she was taken out of Man.'" (Gen. 2:23)

Many people may notice the way Jesus addresses his mother in John as "woman." We may also notice that when St. John wrote the book of revelation we see this term "woman" again. We may notice that in the Gospel and the Apocalypse of St. John it serves as both title and identity, because Mary is not just any woman, she is "THE WOMAN." Just as Christ in not just a man, but the "MAN." the archetype of all men. So too is Mary the archetype of all women. The Gospel of Luke says: "Blessed are you among all women." So, Eve was the first woman, Mary is the final woman. Mary is the completion of the creation of the woman by God. In Christ, man finds his greatest moment. Jesus Christ is the greatest of all men, "For in him the whole fullness of deity dwells bodily." (Col. 2:9) In Mary the creation of woman finds its perfection, and highest point. She is not divine like Jesus, but she is the best of the human race that is pure creature, pure creation. She is the best, the holiest, the greatest, the most humble, and most giving of all men and women, except Jesus. She is the only one besides Christ who is without sin. In the beginning of the world God created a sinless man and woman who fell into sin. In the redemption of the world God brings a new man and woman who never sin and they work together to bring salvation to all those who have sin.

Our prayer reads: "O Mary, Conceived without sin, pray for us who have recourse to thee." In 1830 Mary appeared to St. Catherine Laboure asking for a medal to be made, and promising great graces to those who would wear it around the neck. After the cross, the miraculous medal is the most common Christian necklace in the world. The image of Mary bears a significant resemblance between the woman in Revelation 12. She is clothed with the sun, and rays symbolizing graces fall from her hands. When Mary appeared to St. Bernadette at Lourdes (1858), she revealed her identity with dogma: "I am the Immaculate Conception."

The term "woman" is significant as we follow its use in scripture. We find special significance in Genesis, John, and Revelation. We find a thread in the scriptures between Eve the first "woman" and Mary the new "woman." The term "woman" itself connects and contrasts Mary and Eve, in victory and defeat.

The "Sign" is in Heaven

As we look at chapter 12 in Revelation we see various points for discussion. First we notice the language used in Isaiah is similar:

"Therefore the Lord himself will give you *a sign*. Behold, a young *woman* shall conceive and bear a son, and shall call his name Immanuel." (Is. 7:14)

"And *a great sign* appeared in heaven, a *woman* clothed with the sun, with the moon under her feet, and on her head a crown of twelve stars; {2} she was with child and she cried out in her pangs of birth, in anguish for delivery." (Rev. 12:1, 2)

A Rod of Iron and a Heart of Love

"But one of the soldiers pierced his side with a spear, and at once there came out blood and water." (Jn. 19:34)

The scripture speaks of the Sacred Heart on fire with the love of the world (Jn. 3:16, Mt. 11:29, 15:32), being pierced by an iron rod on the cross. "Behold, he is coming with the clouds, and every eye will see him, every one who pierced him." (Rev. 1:7) When Christ returns he will bring a rod of iron from his throne for those who mocked and rejected his forgiveness and love. We find a reference to the messianic "rod of Iron" in the scriptures. Psalm 2 speaks of the Passion of the Lord when the rulers of church and state who counseled together against Jesus, as they do today. It speaks of how pointless it is to oppose God:

"The kings of the earth set themselves, and the rulers take counsel together, against the Lord and his anointed, saying, {3} 'Let us burst their bonds asunder, and cast their cords from us.' {4} He who sits in the heavens laughs; the Lord has them in derision. {5} Then he will speak to them in his wrath, and terrify them in his fury, saying, {6} 'I have set my king on Zion, my holy hill.' {7} I will tell of the decree of the Lord: He said to me, 'You are my son, today I have begotten you. {8} Ask of me, and I will make the nations your heritage, and the ends of the earth your possession. {9} You shall break them with **a rod of iron.'**" (Ps. 2) "...She brought forth a male child, one who is to rule all the nations with **a rod of iron.**" (Rev. 12:5)

The Ancient Serpent and the New Eve

"In that day the Lord with his hard and great and strong sword will punish Leviathan the fleeing serpent, Leviathan the twisting serpent, and he will slay the dragon that is in the sea." (Is. 27:1)

Although the book of Genesis never calls the serpent the devil in the first few chapters, we find his identity clearly revealed in the book of revelation chapter 12 verse 9:

"And the great dragon was thrown down, that ancient serpent, who is called the Devil and Satan, the deceiver of the whole world—he was thrown down to the earth, and his angels thrown down with him." (Rev. 12:9)

It is interesting to note the comments on this chapter made by John Henry Cardinal Newman. He sees a connection between the revelation of the serpent's identity, along with that of Eve's victorious replacement, the Blessed Virgin Mary:

"The special prerogatives of St. Mary, the *Virgo Virginum*, are intimately involved in the doctrine of the Incarnation itself, with which these remarks began, and have already been dwelt upon above. As is well known, they were not fully recognized in the Catholic ritual till a late date, but they were not a new thing in the Church, or strange to her earlier teachers. St. Justin, St. Irenaeus, and others, had distinctly laid it down, that she not only had an office, but bore a part, and was a voluntary agent, in the actual process of redemption, as Eve had been instrumental and responsible in Adam's fall. They taught that, as the first woman might have foiled the Tempter and did not, so, if Mary had been disobedient or unbelieving on Gabriel's message, the Divine Economy would have been frustrated. And certainly the parallel between 'the Mother of all living' and the Mother of the Redeemer may be gathered from a comparison of the first chapters of scripture with the last. It was noticed in a former place, that the only passage where the serpent is directly identified with the evil spirit occurs in the twelfth chapter of the Revelation; now it is observable that the recognition, when made, is found in the course of a vision of a "woman clothed with the sun and the moon under her feet:" thus two women are brought into contrast with each other. Moreover, as it is said in the Apocalypse, 'The dragon was wroth with the woman, and went about to make war with the remnant of her seed,' so is it prophesied in Genesis, 'I will put enmity between thee and the woman, and between thy seed and her Seed. He shall bruise thy head, and thou shalt bruise His heel.' Also the enmity was to exist, not only between the Serpent and the Seed of the woman, but between the serpent and the woman herself; and here too there is a correspondence in the Apocalyptic vision. If then there is reason for thinking that this mystery at the close of the Scripture record answers to the mystery in the beginning of it, and that 'the Woman' mentioned in both passages is one and the same, then she can be none other than St. Mary, thus introduced prophetically to our notice immediately on the transgression of Eve."(An Essay on the Development of Christian Doctrine, by John Henry Cardinal Newman, Christian Classics Inc. Westminster, MO, 1968, pp. 415, 416.)

We see further verses which are difficult to understand that speak of the dragon pursuing the woman:

"And when the dragon saw that he had been thrown down to the earth, he pursued the woman who had borne the male child. {14} But the woman was given the two wings of the great eagle that she might fly from the serpent into the wilderness, to the place where she is to be nourished for a time, and times, and half a time." (Rev. 12:13-14)

This passage refers to the woman getting the two wings of an eagle which could be a symbolic pointing towards how she was lifted up from the sins of men, and remained sinless although she was flesh like the rest of men. The reference to being raised up on eagle's wings may also be a symbolic allusion to the end of her life when she was assumed body and soul into heaven. In scripture we see other lesser figures like Elijah and others (Gen. 5:24, 2K. 2, Mt. 17:2, 27:53, Heb. 11:5, 6) being assumed into heaven so how much more should she who the Holy Spirit says is "blessed among all women." (Lk. 2)   In the scriptures we see how the reference to the eagle's wings refers to God's protection:

"You have seen what I did to the Egyptians, and how I bore you on eagles' wings and brought you to myself." (Ex. 19:4)

"He found him in a desert land, and in the howling waste of the wilderness; he encircled him, he cared for him, he kept him as the apple of his eye. {11} Like an eagle that stirs up its nest, that flutters over its young, spreading out its wings, catching them, bearing them on its pinions, {12} the Lord alone did lead him, and there was no foreign god with him. {13} He made him ride on the high places of the earth, and he ate the produce of the field; and he made him suck honey out of the rock, and oil out of the flinty rock. {14} Curds from the herd, and milk from the flock, with fat of lambs and rams, herds of Bashan and goats, with the finest of the wheat—and of the blood of the grape you drank wine." (Deut. 32:10-14)

"But they who wait for the Lord shall renew their strength, they shall mount up with wings like eagles, they shall run and not be weary, they shall walk and not faint." (Is. 40:31)

"He who dwells in the shelter of the Most High, who abides in the shadow of the Almighty, {2} will say to the Lord, 'My refuge and my fortress; my God, in whom I trust.' {3} For he will deliver you from the snare of the fowler and from the deadly pestilence; {4} he will cover you with his pinions, and under his wings you will find refuge; his faithfulness is a shield and buckler.'" (Ps. 81:1-4)

"O that I had wings like a dove! I would fly away and be at rest; {7} yea, I would wander afar, I would lodge in the wilderness, [Selah] {8} I would haste to find me a shelter from the raging wind and tempest." (Ps. 55:6)

So it is clear that the woman in Revelation 12 is protected by God from the dragon, as ancient Israel was led across the desert away from Egypt. Just as there was a little Exodus that Jesus, Mary and Joseph went on:

"And he rose and took the child and his mother by night, and departed to Egypt, {15} and remained there until the death of Herod. This was to fulfill what the Lord had spoken by the prophet, 'Out of Egypt have I called my son.'" (Mt. 2:14)

As the story of the Dragon pursuing the woman continues we see a reference to water which we saw used by God against the people in the day of Noah, and the pursuing Egyptians in Exodus:

"Then the Lord said to Moses, 'Stretch out your hand over the sea, that the water may come back upon the Egyptians, upon their chariots, and upon their horsemen.' {27} So Moses stretched forth his hand over the sea, and the sea returned to its wonted flow when the morning appeared; and the Egyptians fled into it, and the Lord routed the Egyptians in the midst of the sea. {28} The waters returned and covered the chariots and the horsemen and all the host of Pharaoh that had followed them into the sea; not so much as one of them remained. {29} But the people of Israel walked on dry ground through the sea, the waters being a wall to them on their right hand and on their left. {30} Thus the Lord saved Israel that day from the hand of the Egyptians; and Israel saw the Egyptians dead upon the seashore. {31} And Israel saw the great work which the Lord did against the Egyptians, and the people feared the Lord; and they believed in the Lord and in his servant Moses.'" (Ex. 14:26-31)

So we keep Exodus 14 above as the background as read on in Revelation 12. Just as the waters were taken away to protect ancient Israel so they could pass to the promised land, so too was the Woman protected from the waters, that she might pass through the desert to the true promised land of heaven. The dragon could not harm the woman, so he was angry:

"The serpent poured water like a river out of his mouth after the woman, to sweep her away with the flood. {16} But the earth came to the help of the woman, and the earth opened its mouth and swallowed the river which the dragon had poured from his mouth. {17} Then the dragon was angry with the woman, and went off to make war on the rest of her offspring, on those who keep the commandments of God and bear testimony to Jesus. And he stood on the sand of the sea." (Rev. 12:15-17)

So the sea takes away the breath of those it drowns, but the woman is protected from the dragon's attacks and escapes. In Isaiah we see some interestingly similar references to the dragon and the water which the redeemed pass over:

"...My deliverance will be for ever, and my salvation to all generations." {9} Awake, awake, put on strength, O arm of the Lord; awake, as in days of old, the generations of long ago. Was it not thou that didst cut Rahab in pieces, that didst pierce the dragon? {10} Was it not thou that didst dry up the sea, the waters of the great deep; that didst make the depths of the sea a way for the redeemed to pass over?" (Is. 51:8-10)

So we see many symbols of the Old Testament coming together with Mary. Just as ancient Israel was delivered from its enemies which were ultimately forces of the devil, so too is Mary the Mother of Jesus, ultimately delivered from the devil and sin. So the devil seeks to make war against the rest of her offspring, namely the members of the Church.

The Cloth of Guadalupe and the Woman in the Apocalypse

"Greet Mary, who has worked hard among you." (Rom. 16:6)

From her Immaculate Conception to her Heavenly Coronation, Mary has labored hard in the vineyard of this world for the salvation of her spiritual children. The work of Mary from beginning to end is the Evangelization of the world. From the moment she said "Yes" to being the Mother of God, to the moment she appeared on the hill in Guadalupe, her mission is to bring Christ to the world. From the moment the Angel appeared to her, to the moment she appeared to Juan Diego her mission is to help the world love Christ, through her obedience to God (Lk. 1:38) and through her requests to God on our behalf. (Jn. 2:3)

Looking at the comments of the Popes and others over the years regarding the identity of the Woman with Mary and the Church, I wish to make another more external point. I wish to point out that we see a similarity between the Woman in chapter 12 of the Book of Revelation and the Woman on the Cloth of Guadalupe. The woman in the image on the Cloth of Guadalupe is pregnant, as is the woman in Revelation 12. The woman on the cloth is clothed with the sun and has the moon under her feet just like the woman in Revelation 12. The Cloth of Guadalupe is an extraordinary thing, having been analyzed by scientists and found to have mysterious properties similar to those of the shroud of Turin. It is my opinion that the similarities between the cloth of Guadalupe and the Woman in Revelation 12 are one of God's ways of showing us that the woman in Revelation 12 is Mary the Mother of Jesus.

So, it seems we have established that the Woman in Revelation 12 is a layered symbolism for ancient Israel and the Church, but is primarily Mary since she is the best disciple of Jesus from both Israel and the Church, both Old Covenant under which she was born, and the New Covenant which she lived and was assumed into heaven. So Christ is the King born under the Old Covenant who brought us the new Covenant, and he is the head of the Church. And, Mary is the Queen Mother born under the Old Covenant who gave birth to Christ the King and His mystical body the Church, the rest of her offspring. Revelation 12 makes it clear that since she "wears a crown of twelve stars" she is a Queen, and it describes her as the mother who gives birth to Christ and "those who give witness to Jesus." Mary is the New Eve, the Queen of Heaven, and the Mother of the Church, the "mother of all the living." (Gen. 3:20)

Chapter 5

The Assumption of Mary

"...many bodies of the saints who had fallen asleep were raised, and coming out of the tombs after his resurrection they went into the holy city and appeared to many." (Mt. 27:51-53)

We see in scripture that others shared in a bodily assumption, so how much more she who gave birth to the body of Christ deserves such a gift! On November 1, 1950, *Pope Pius XII* declared the Dogma of the Assumption of Mary:

"By the authority of our Lord Jesus Christ, of the Blessed Apostles Peter and Paul, and by our own authority, we pronounce, declare, and define it to be a divinely revealed dogma: that the Immaculate Mother of God, the ever Virgin Mary, having completed the course of her earthly life, was assumed body and soul into heavenly glory." (Constitution *Munificentissimus Deus*, no. 44)

We see throughout scripture select saints have been given special privileges and honors. We see some who have a mysterious type of early sharing in the resurrection before the general judgment at the end of the world. Scripture says:

"Enoch walked with God; and he was not, for God took him." (Gen. 5:24)

"No one like Enoch has been created on earth, for he was taken up from the earth." (Sir. 49:14)

"And as they still went on and talked, behold, a chariot of fire and horses of fire separated the two of them. And Elijah went up by a whirlwind into heaven." (2K. 2:11)

"By faith Enoch was taken up so that he should not see death; and he was not found, because God had taken him. Now before he was taken he was attested as having pleased God." (Heb. 11:5)

"But when the archangel Michael, contending with the devil, disputed about the body of Moses, he did not presume to pronounce a reviling judgment upon him, but said, 'The Lord rebuke you.'" (Jude 9)

"And behold, two men talked with him, Moses and Elijah, {31} who appeared in glory and spoke of his departure, which he was to accomplish at Jerusalem." (Lk. 9:30) [Notice the scripture says Moses and Elijah appeared "in glory," how much more glory does Mary appear with in Heaven than Moses and Elijah!]

"And behold, the curtain of the temple was torn in two, from top to bottom; and the earth shook, and the rocks were split; {52} the tombs also were opened, and *many bodies of the saints who had fallen asleep were raised,* {53} and coming out of the tombs after his resurrection they went into the holy city *and appeared to many*." (Mt. 27:51-53) [Notice that they '*appeared to many*' showing a biblical basis for Marian Apparitions like Guadalupe, Lourdes, and Fatima.]

Notice what the scripture says about the bodies of other saints being preserved and glorified, how much more she who conceived by the Holy Spirit and was blessed among all women! Could she who was the spouse of the Holy Spirit, she from whose body Our Lord derived his body, be left to rot in the earth? When lesser saints have had their bodies spared corruption, how much more fitting it is for she who is "Blessed among all women" to have her body taken up to heaven with her son who is Blessed among all men! Christ is the new Adam, who never sinned, Mary is the new Eve, who never sinned. She has been assumed body and soul into heaven, and sits at the right hand of her son in glory. May we honor His mother Mary as he does, and he will bless us for imitating him.

God the Father honors her, God the Son honors her, God the Holy Spirit honors her, and we the Church, the body of Christ, honor her as our mother! Each day all over the world the mystical body of Christ honors Mary with millions of Rosaries!

Chapter 6

The Intercession of Mary

"And the king rose to meet her, and bowed down to her; then he sat on his throne, and had a seat brought for the king's mother; and she sat on his right." (1K. 2:19)

Parallels between Queen Mary and Queen Bathsheba

King Solomon was the Son of David, and prefigured Christ who would be called the Son of David and fulfill the Messianic prophesies of Glory for the Son of David.

"Once for all I have sworn by my holiness; I will not lie to David. {36} His line shall endure for ever, his throne as long as the sun before me." (Ps. 89:35-36)

King Solomon's Queen was not his wife, but his mother. Bathsheba was the Queen Mother of Israel. She was the mother of the Son of David, she was the Queen who sat next to her son and asked favors and interceded with her son King Solomon on behalf of the people of Israel. Although the particular request recorded in scripture is a trick which seeks to use Solomon's mother against him, and is exposed by the wisdom of Solomon, we see from this passage the intercessory role played by the Queen Mother. We can tell from this passage that the role of the Queen Mother as intercessor with her son the king is clearly established. And, this event in the earthly Jerusalem with the son of David, is a foreshadowing of what happens in the heavenly Jerusalem with the Divine Son of David. Bathsheba is the Queen Mother with the Son of David in the earthly Jerusalem; Mary is the Queen Mother in the Heavenly Jerusalem. (Rev. 21:2) Scripture says:

"So Solomon sat upon the throne of David his father; and his kingdom was firmly established. {13} Then Adonijah the son of Haggith came to Bathsheba the mother of Solomon. And she said, 'Do you come peaceably?' He said, 'Peaceably.' {14} Then he said, 'I have something to say to you.' She said, 'Say on.' {15} He said, 'You know that the kingdom was mine, and that all Israel fully expected me to reign; however the kingdom has turned about and become my brothers, for it was his from the Lord. {16} And now I have one request to make of you; do not refuse me.' She said to him, 'Say on.' {17} And he said, '***Pray ask*** King Solomon—he will not refuse you—to give me Abishag the Shunammite as my wife.' {18} Bathsheba said, 'Very well; I will speak for you to the king.' {19} So Bathsheba went to King Solomon, to speak to him on behalf of Adonijah. ***And the king rose to meet her, and bowed down to her; then he sat on his throne, and had a seat brought for the king's mother; and she sat on his right.*** {20} Then she said, 'I have one small request to make of you; do not refuse me.' And the king said to her, '***Make your request, my mother; for I will not refuse you.***'" (1K. 2)

In a way similar to Bathsheba, Mary is the Mother of Jesus Christ, the Son of David. In fact the first line of the New Testament begins, "*The* book of the genealogy of Jesus Christ, the son of David." (Mt. 1:1) Mary asks for favors and intercedes with her Son Jesus on behalf of the people of Israel, the wedding guests at Cana. (Jn. 2) ***Make your request, my mother; for I will not refuse you.*** (1K. 2) Bathsheba was forgiven by God for sins of adultery and granted a second son, Solomon, who was born in wedlock to replace the child conceived in adultery. Mary would have been a sinner if Jesus had not prevented it at her conception. So, both Mary and Bathsheba are saved by God from sin, but in two different ways.

The envious woman in Luke 11:27, and the ambitious apostles sought the honor of Mary. Jesus says the seat at his right in his kingdom is reserved by the Father. Note that the mother of Zebedee here intercedes on behalf of her sons! How traditional and biblical is the intercession of a mother! Scripture says:

"Then the mother of the sons of Zebedee came up to him, with her sons, and kneeling before him she asked him for something. {21} And he said to her, 'What do you want?' She said to him, 'Command that these two sons of mine may sit, one at your right hand and one at your left, in your kingdom.' {22} But Jesus answered, 'You do not know what you are asking. Are you able to drink the cup that I am to drink?' They said to him, 'We are able.' {23} He said to them, 'You will drink my cup, but to sit at my right hand and at my left is not mine to grant, but it is for those for whom it has been prepared by my Father.' {24} And when the ten heard it, they were indignant at the two brothers." (Mt. 20:20-24)

The Holy Spirit speaks through St. Elizabeth:

"{41} And when Elizabeth heard the greeting of Mary, the babe leaped in her womb; and Elizabeth was filled with the Holy Spirit {42} and she exclaimed with a loud cry, *'Blessed are you among women, and blessed is the fruit of your womb!* {43} And why is this granted me, that the mother of my Lord should come to me?'" (Lk. 1:41-43)

We believe the seat at his right hand is given by God to her who is blessed among all women. She is also blessed among all men except Jesus. The highest seat in heaven goes to the most humble and most holy Virgin Mary, her own words indicate this:

"And Mary said, 'My soul magnifies the Lord, {47} and my spirit rejoices in God my Savior, {48} for he has regarded the low estate of his handmaiden. For behold, henceforth all generations will call me blessed; {49} for he who is mighty has done great things for me, and holy is his name. {50} And his mercy is on those who fear him from generation to generation. {51} He has shown strength with his arm, he has scattered the proud in the imagination of their hearts, {52} he has put down the mighty from their thrones, and exalted those of low degree...'" (Lk. 1:46-52)

In the earthly court of the earthly Jerusalem, we saw the Queen Mother Bathsheba sitting and interceding at the right hand of her Son the King, the son of David. In the court of the Heavenly Jerusalem (Rev.

21:10) we have Mary the Queen Mother sitting and interceding at the right hand of her son the King of Kings, the son of David. Mary is the Queen Mother of Heaven and Earth, she is the Queen of Queens and her Son who gives the highest honor to his Mother is the King of Kings!

Pope Pius XII wrote: "...as Queen, she sits in splendor at the right hand of her Son, the immortal King." (*Munificentissimus Deus*)

To those who seek to deny honor to the Blessed Virgin Mary I ask this question: "If you don't believe Mary is the one seated at the right hand of her Son Jesus in the Kingdom of Heaven, who is it that you think is sitting there?! Who does scripture indicate is more worthy of this seat than Mary??!!!" Someone is there since Our Lord says:

"...to sit at my right hand and at my left is not mine to grant, but it is for those for whom it has been prepared by my Father." (Mt. 20:23)

As Catholics we believe that Mary was prepared by the Father at her Immaculate Conception to be the one seated at the right hand of Christ in glory. As Catholics we believe St. Joseph was prepared by the Father to represent God the Father on earth, as the foster father of Jesus, and to be at seated at the left hand of Jesus in glory.

I think part of the root of the problem with people who don't like devotion to Mary is pride. They don't want to admit that there is someone who served God better than everyone else, and that God has chosen to honor them for it as a means of helping us. The whole of scripture is full of stories of people who served God better than we did, and they form examples for us to look up to, and honor, and imitate. Of all those who served God, Mary is the greatest servant of all. Many times we hear it said, "Why do Catholics talk so much about Mary? Why don't they just talk about Jesus. In my spiritual life it's just me and Jesus!" There is a problem with that. God gives us our neighbor to help us love him, and to share his love with each other. How would it be if we went to church on Sunday and we were the only ones there? Isn't it better to have a church full of people praising God with me? Doesn't their presence and example help me love God and my neighbor better? Maybe the universe isn't just "Me and Jesus." The universe is actually Jesus, my neighbor, and me! And we certainly have a lot of neighbors. So out of all our neighbors, the first ones in priority are our parents. We need to remember that in the Ten Commandments the first three deal with the love of God, and the next seven deal with the love of neighbor. And, the first of the seven that deal with the love of neighbor start with honoring our parents. They are first in the line of neighbors. So God is teaching us something right there. The first commandment that deals with our neighbor is to honor our father and mother. So our parents are the first to help us love God by their words, prayers, and example. We watch them pray, and we learn to pray, and we want to pray with them. They pray with us, and they pray for us. So God has given us neighbors to help us grow in the love of God, and to help us get to heaven. In the line of neighbor the first is our parents. Mary is our maternal spiritual parent. So too, in the line of saints, the first in line is Mary, who is "Blessed among all women." Mary is our spiritual Mother. She gave birth to the body of Christ, and the church is the spiritual or mystical body of Christ. So she is the mystical or spiritual mother of all the children of God. She is the "New Eve," as it says of Eve, "...She became the mother of all the living." So, too, Mary is the replacement for Eve. At the foot of the Cross, Christ said, "Woman, behold your Son," and "Behold your mother." Thus, in the act of conceiving by the Holy Spirit, she became the mother of God the Son. Since only those with Christ dwelling in them are spiritually alive, so too, those who are one with Christ, have Mary as their mother. When we receive the body and blood of Christ in the Eucharist, we are joined to him physically and spiritually. We become sons of the Father and sons of Mary. Mary is the Mother of Christ; Mary is the mother of all the sons of God. So, through this process of entering the family of God as the mother of God she became the "mother of all the living."

She entered the Family of God in a different way than we do. She still enters through union with Christ, but she is conceived without sin and then she conceives by the Holy Spirit. She is unique. She is set apart by God from among all the saints. She is the first among those saved in Christ. She was the first to touch Him, the first to believe in Him, and the first to be redeemed by Him. She is preeminent among all neighbors on a spiritual level, just as Eve was preeminent among all our neighbors on a physical level. Eve is the mother of us all physically. Mary is the mother of us all spiritually. The Ark of the Old Covenant was made of wood and gold. The ark of the new covenant is made of flesh and blood. The contents of the ark of the old covenant were stone, manna, and the rod of Aaron. The contents of the ark of the new covenant are the body and blood of Christ, the living manna come from heaven, Jesus Christ the High priest who is also the victim lamb of God.

Mary is the Ark of the New Covenant. The New Covenant is the body and blood of Christ. For nine months Jesus was protected in the holy womb of Mary. Then he was born into the world to die in sacrifice on the cross. Mary not only gave birth to the Head of the mystical Body of Christ, she gave birth to the members as well. She is the Queen Mother, she is the New Eve, she is the Ark of the Covenant. Mary is the Mystical Ark of the Mystical body of Christ, namely the Church.

The Wedding, the Wine and the Miracle

"Make your request, my mother; for I will not refuse you."
(1K. 2:19, 20)

In the scripture we see the kingly court of Solomon in Jerusalem. It is a foreshadowing of the heavenly court. King Solomon, the son of David is a symbol for Christ the King. The Queen Mother Bathsheba is a symbol for Mary the Queen of Heaven. The Queen sits at the right of her son to bring requests from subjects. In the Old Testament story the request is not granted because the request is made in a act of treachery which deceives the Queen, but not King Solomon. He sees that his enemies are abusing his mother's normal role as an advocate. Nevertheless, we see this role as advocate shown on the earthly court of King Solomon as a reflection of the heavenly court of Christ the King of Heaven, where His Mother sits at his right as Queen of heaven. Regarding the role of advocate we see the King honor his mother and desire to grant her request:

"And the king rose to meet her, and bowed down to her; then he sat on his throne, and had a seat brought for the king's mother; and she sat on his right. {20} Then she said, 'I have one small request to make of you; do not refuse me.' And the king said to her, 'Make your request, my mother; for I will not refuse you.'" (1K. 2:19, 20)

We see a similar event occur in the beginning of the Gospel, where Jesus grants the request of Mary his mother at the wedding of Cana. We must note that this wedding marks the beginning of Jesus' public ministry. So the fact that it is a wedding points toward the wedding of the groom Christ, and his bride the church:

"And I saw the holy city, new Jerusalem, coming down out of heaven from God, prepared as a bride adorned for her husband." (Rev. 21:2)

"For the husband is the head of the wife as Christ is the head of the church, his body, and is himself its Savior. ...{29} For no man ever hates his own flesh, but nourishes and cherishes it, as Christ does the church, {30} because we are members of his body. {31} For this reason a man shall leave his father and mother and be joined to his wife, and the two shall become one flesh. {32} *This mystery is a profound one, and I am saying that it refers to Christ and the church;* {33} however, let each one of you love his wife as himself, and let the wife see that she respects her husband." (Eph. 5:23-32)

"And Jesus said to them, 'Can the wedding guests fast while the bridegroom is with them? As long as they have the bridegroom with them, they cannot fast. {20} The days will come, when the bridegroom is taken away from them, and then they will fast in that day.'" (Mk. 2:19-20)

"And again Jesus spoke to them in parables, saying, {2} 'The kingdom of heaven may be compared to a king who gave a marriage feast for his son, {3} and sent his servants to call those who were invited to the marriage feast...' Then he said to his servants, 'The wedding is ready, but those invited were not worthy. {9} Go therefore to the thoroughfares, and invite to the marriage feast as many as you find.' {10} And those servants went out into the streets and gathered all whom they found, both bad and good." (Mt. 22:1-10)

In scripture we see the mysterious "hour" (Jn. 2:4, 12:27, 13:1) of the first miracle and what it reveals about Jesus and Mary. Also, Mary was there at his "first hour" which began with the Incarnation at the Annunciation, and Mary was there at the foot of the cross during his "final hour" of the Redemption.   In John Chapter 2 Jesus works his first miracle and it is recorded in scripture as happening through the intercession of Mary with her son to create more wine. In this miracle we also see a foreshadowing of the last miracle he works at the end of his ministry in the presence of his disciples, at the last supper. There he turns wine into his precious blood, and this is the transition point between his public ministry and his sacrificial passion. So his ministry begins with making wine to increase the joy of the wedding feast, and his ministry ends with turning wine into his precious blood to enable the wedding feast of the kingdom of heaven. He does this to win his bride from sin so there can be a wedding between Christ and his bride—the Church. So the wine points to the joy of the wedding. The last supper, and the passion on the cross which brings about the union with the bride the Church, as he sacrifices his life to save his bride the Church.

Notice Mary doesn't say, "They have no wine, please work a miracle and get them wine." She simply says: "They have no wine." The implication is clear. She says this to Jesus because she knows he can do something, and she is clearly asking him. Jesus responds with a strange question regarding what this has to do with him, and that his hour has not yet come. Yet, his actions reveal that these words are deeper and more mysterious. For he works the miracle that she asks for, so his response that on the surface sounds like a "no" cannot possibly be a "no." For our Lord would not say "no" to Mary's request, and then say "yes" by doing it. So, we must reflect that this response of Jesus contains a greater mystery. So, how can we seek to understand it? His response seems to be this problem is not our concern, his hour has not yet come. However, it is through Mary's yes at the Annunciation that his first hour on earth began in her womb. Now it is through Mary's words of implied request that the countdown to his last hour begins. Mary knows that this miracle of wine will manifest him as the Messiah to his disciples and others at the wedding, and begin the final countdown of hours to his passion, death, and resurrection. This was why he came, to give his life as a sacrifice. In this humble little setting at the wedding of Cana his public ministry as the miracle working messiah begins. In the humble setting of Mary's house the Archangel Gabriel came to announce that she was chosen to be the Mother of God. In the humble setting of Bethlehem, in a manger, the Son of God was born. In the humble setting of the wedding at Cana, Jesus worked his first public miracle through the intercession of his mother. God chose it to be this way, Mary co-operated with God's providential choice. Mary's consent at the Annunciation brought Christ the light into this world. It was no accident that Mary's request ignited the light of the world. The public ministry of Jesus was to begin through his first public miracle. Scripture clearly mentions this as his first miracle, that it manifested his glory, and that the effect was that his disciples believed in him. "This, the first of his signs, Jesus did at Cana in Galilee, and manifested his glory; and his disciples believed in him." (Jn. 2:11) Mary now continues this work in heaven, that through her intercession, she helps his disciples believe in him, and he manifests his glory through her intercession. He has chosen to link his hour with her hour. It has been this way since the beginning of his life in her womb. His request at the Annunciation brought her "yes," now her request at the wedding of Cana for the first public miracle brought his "yes"!

The first stage of redemption, the Incarnation, involved Mary's response. Mary's response to the Father's request begins his life as man and mission as redeemer. Mary said, "Let it be done to me according to your word." (Lk. 1:38) For this hour of the first miracle begins his final stage of life as the miracle working messiah, and this hour begins Mary's final stage of intercessor for the people of God with her son Jesus. Her next spiritual role is that of prayer intercessor with Jesus on behalf of her people, her spiritual children. We see this "hour" is not just "his hour," but "their hour." He says, "O woman, what have you to do with me? *My hour* has not yet come." (Jn. 2:4) Just as his first hour of incarnation came through her participation, so now his first hour as

Miracle Working Messiah comes with her participation as well. This is his hour to show his power, and this is her hour to show her special relationship as Queen Mother and intercessor. This is our hour where we recognize Mary's mysterious role as our spiritual helpmate in God's plan of salvation. So, this is Mary's hour because Jesus honors his mother by granting her request. The honor seems even more since he seemed reluctant to do it, but the power of his mother's intercession is thus manifested, and in this event we see her glory alongside and supporting his glory. For the mother prepares her son for the wedding. So Mary prepares her son Jesus for his bride the Church by prompting him to manifest his glory and starting the inaugural process of his Kingdom. Scripture sees a foreshadowing of this in King Solomon, who is a type of Christ as the son of David. It says: "...behold King Solomon, with the crown with which his mother crowned him on the day of his wedding, on the day of the gladness of his heart."(Song of Songs 3:11)

In addition to the interesting symbolism of the wedding, the wine, and the miracle, we must also note the time. As we read the passage we must remember that the number three is a symbol for the trinity, that Jesus rises on the third day. The scripture speaks about the third day as a significant day regarding the manifestation of Christ's glory:

"At that very hour some Pharisees came, and said to him, 'Get away from here, for Herod wants to kill you.' {32} And he said to them, Go and tell that fox, *Behold, I cast out demons and perform cures today and tomorrow, and the **third day** I finish my course.*" (Lk. 13:31-32)

"The Son of man must suffer many things, and be rejected by the elders and chief priests and scribes, and be killed, and on the *third day* be raised." (Lk. 9:22)

"While they were perplexed about this, behold, two men stood by them in dazzling apparel; {5} and as they were frightened and bowed their faces to the ground, the men said to them, 'Why do you seek the living among the dead? He is not here, but has risen.' {6} 'Remember how he told you, while he was still in Galilee, {7} that the Son of man must be delivered into the hands of sinful men, and be crucified, and on *the third day* rise.'" (Lk. 24:4-7)

"Come, let us return to the Lord; for he has torn, that he may heal us; he has stricken, and he will bind us up. {2} After two days he will revive us; on *the third day* he will raise us up, that we may live before him." (Hosea 6:1, 2)

So as we read John 2 we note that it mentions this occurs on the third day. Scripture says:

"On *the third day* there was a marriage at Cana in Galilee, and the mother of Jesus was there; {2} Jesus also was invited to the marriage, with his disciples. {3} When the wine failed, the mother of Jesus said to him, 'They have no wine.' {4} And Jesus said to her, 'O woman, what have you to do with me? My hour has not yet come.' {5} His mother said to the servants, 'Do whatever he tells you.' {6} Now six stone jars were standing there, for the Jewish rites of purification, each holding twenty or thirty gallons. {7} Jesus said to them, 'Fill the jars with water.' And they filled them up to the brim. {8} He said to them, 'Now draw some out, and take it to the steward of the feast.' So they took it. {9} When the steward of the feast tasted the water now become wine, and did not know where it came from (though the servants who had drawn the water knew), the steward of the feast called the bridegroom {10} and said to him, "Every man serves the good wine first; and when men have drunk freely, then the poor wine; but you have kept the good wine until now.' {11} *This, the first of his signs, Jesus did at Cana in Galilee, and manifested his glory; and his disciples believed in him.*" (Jn. 2:1-11)

Here we see the first hint of the new role of Mary as the grandest of all human intercessors with her son, in the first place of all the saints, "Blessed are you among all women." (Lk. 1:42) We can pray for each other on earth, and we can join our prayers on earth to Mary's in heaven. The intercession of Mary with her son Jesus brought joy and gladness to the guests at Cana, and we on earth who ask her prayers in heaven today are also gladdened and joyful with her spiritual aid.

"Who has not returned to everyday life gladdened and joyful because his request had been granted by the Mother of God?" (The Liturgy of the Hours, Vol. IV, Catholic Book Publishing Co. N.Y., 1975, copyright ICEL 1970,1973,1975, Office of readings "From a homily by Saint Amadeus of Lausanne, bishop." Vol. IV. pg 1339)

"After the Lord had spoken these words to Job, the Lord said to

Eliphaz the Temanite: 'My wrath is kindled against you and against your two friends; for you have not spoken of me what is right, as my servant Job has. {8} Now therefore take seven bulls and seven rams, and go to my servant Job, and offer up for yourselves a burnt offering; and *my servant Job shall pray for you, for I will accept his prayer not to deal with you according to your folly; for you have not spoken of me what is right, as my servant Job has.'* {9} So Eliphaz the Temanite and Bildad the Shuhite and Zophar the Naamathite went and did what the Lord had told them; and the Lord accepted Job's prayer. {10} And the Lord restored the fortunes of Job, when he had prayed for his friends; and the Lord gave Job twice as much as he had before." (Job 42:7-10)

"The prayer of a righteous man has great power in its effects. Elijah was a man of like nature with ourselves and he prayed fervently that it might not rain, and for three years and six months it did not rain on the earth. Then he prayed again and the heaven gave rain, and the earth brought forth its fruit." (Jam. 5:16-18)

If the prayers of Job and Elijah were so powerful how much greater are those of the Blessed Virgin Mary! We have the greatest and most faithful servant of God available to offer her prayers for our soul, for Mary is greater than Elijah and Job! So great is the love of God that he gives us the prayers of his Mother as a gift to those who honor her! What are the riches of this world compared to the gift of the prayers of the Mother of God! We need no money, no fame, no special alliance, to avail ourselves of the prayers of the Queen of Heaven, for she herself said: "he has put down the mighty from their thrones, and exalted those of low degree." (Lk. 1:52) A poor man with his Rosary has greater riches than a rich man with his money. For we know that the money of this world is temporary, but the riches of heaven are eternal. The Rosary makes a poor sinner a friend of the Queen of Heaven, and she helps him through the gates to paradise.

We must remember however, not all prayers are answered with a yes. The answers God gives to prayer are as follows: yes, no, and please wait. Sometimes it is hard to tell the difference between no and please wait, but if a time factor is involved in the request this too becomes clear. Prayers are answered according to God's individual master plan for our salvation. This plan is also changing constantly according to our individual responses to his daily offers to grow in grace and do battle with temptations.

So, unfortunately, there are times when God does say no to our requests in prayers to escape sufferings. He does this for our own good in his master plan for our salvation. We may not always understand, but we must continue to trust. In this mysterious answer to St. Paul I believe our Lord also speaks to us all regarding the times our prayer request is denied. Even the great St. Paul was denied his request:

"And to keep me from being too elated by the abundance of revelations, a thorn was given me in the flesh, a messenger of Satan, to harass me, to keep me from being too elated. {8} *Three times I besought the Lord about this, that it should leave me; {9} but he said to me, 'My grace is sufficient for you, for my power is made perfect in weakness.'* I will all the more gladly boast of my weaknesses, that the power of Christ may rest upon me. {10} For the sake of Christ, then, I am content with weaknesses, insults, hardships, persecutions, and calamities; for when I am weak, then I am strong." (2Cor. 12:7-10)

Mary: The Mirror of God

And Mary said, "My soul magnifies the Lord."
(Lk. 1:46)

A mirror is not the source of light, but if it is pure and clean it can reflect the light and focus it in an area. Just as the moon reflects the light of the sun at night, so too, Mary reflects the light of God. The scripture speaks of this in a similar way with the dream of Joseph which compares his father to the sun and his mother to the moon:

"Then he dreamed another dream, and told it to his brothers, and said, 'Behold, I have dreamed another dream; and behold, the sun, the moon, and eleven stars were bowing down to me.' {10} But when he told it to his father and to his brothers, his father rebuked him, and said to him, 'What is this dream that you have dreamed? Shall I and your mother and your brothers indeed come to bow ourselves to the ground before you?' {11} And his brothers were jealous of him, but his father kept the saying in mind." (Gen. 37:9-11)

His dream forms the basis of a sort of theological cosmology; an analogy of theological truths which use the stars, moon, and sun. The moon does not produce its own light, but takes the light of the sun and uses it to light up the darkness of the night. The moon is like a giant mirror in the sky that reflects the light of the sun into the darkness of the night sky. Like the moon clothed with the light of the sun at night, Mary reflects the Light of her Son upon the world. Like a giant mirror which magnifies and focuses the light of the sun, her "soul magnifies the Lord." (Lk. 1:46) She is like "a woman, clothed with the Sun, with the moon under her feet." (Rev. 12:1) As the only sinless disciple and the spouse of the Holy Spirit, I believe the Song of Songs makes allusions to the beauty of her soul. Scripture says:

"Whither has your beloved gone, O *fairest among women*? ... {9} My dove, my perfect one, is only one, the darling of her mother, *flawless to her that bore her.* The maidens saw her and called her happy; the queens and concubines also, and they praised her. {10} 'Who is this that looks forth like the dawn, *fair as the moon, bright as the sun,* terrible as an army with banners?' How graceful are your feet in sandals, *O queenly maiden!"* (Song of Songs 6:1, 9-11, 7:1)

Of all the lights that light up the night sky the brightest is the moon. It is brighter than all the stars of the sky. In Joseph's dream we see his brothers compared to the other stars. So too, Mary reflects the light of God more than all the other saints or children of God. The stars in the night are like the saints in heaven, but the moon is like Mary. The moon produces so much more light than any other star, and Mary helps us love God more than any other saint. Speaking of the glory of the body in the resurrection St. Paul makes reference to the stars:

"And what you sow is not the body which is to be, but a bare kernel, perhaps of wheat or of some other grain. {38} But God gives it a body as he has chosen, and to each kind of seed its own body. {39} For not all flesh is alike, but there is one kind for men, another for animals, another for birds, and another for fish. {40} *There are celestial bodies and there are terrestrial bodies; but the glory of the celestial is one, and the glory of the terrestrial is another. {41} There is one glory of the sun, and another glory of the moon, and another glory of the stars; for star differs from star in glory. {42}* So is it with the resurrection of the dead. What is sown is perishable, what is raised is imperishable. {43} It is sown in dishonor, it is raised in glory. It is sown in weakness, it is raised in power. {44} It is sown a physical body, it is raised a spiritual body. If there is a physical body, there is also a spiritual body." (1Cor. 15:37-44)

"And those who are wise shall shine like the brightness of the firmament; and those who turn many to righteousness, *like the stars for ever* and ever." (Dan. 12:3)

Interesting to note that the Cloth of Guadalupe has stars on the robe of Mary which reflect accurately the constellations in the sky at that place and time.

The Worship of God and the Honor of Mary

"For Behold, henceforth all generations will call me blessed." (Lk. 1:48)

The difference between worship and honor is often confusing. Worship is the highest form of honor, veneration, praise, esteem, and glory that men can give and it is reserved to God alone. However, God does expect us to honor each other, especially our parents. They in turn teach us to love and worship God. There is a great difference between the honor, praise, and glory we give to God and that we give to our parents, the saints, and other humans. The honor we give to men is limited, partial, and incomplete because the good we derive from our neighbors originates in God and is designed to help lead us to worship Him. So, before we learn to worship, love, honor, and obey God, we learn to love, honor, and obey our parents who represent him to us as children. They in turn teach us to love, honor, and obey God which is a praiseworthy deed. The saints, who are our elder servants in the Lord, also teach us to love God by their words and deeds, and so we honor the saints as well. *'Remember your leaders, who spoke to you the word of God. Consider how they ended their lives, and imitate their faith.'* (Heb. 13:7) Their deeds are in scripture and in the lives of the saints. God honors and rewards our parents and the saints for helping us to love him. So the love and honor goes throughout the family of God, from the greatest to the least. The honor we give to Mary is the highest of all the saints, because of her pre-eminent role as the Queen and Mother in the family of God.

Like a good mother she watches over us to help us with her prayers. Like good children we honor and love our mother, for she leads us to God. This is why our Lord said, "Behold your mother." (Jn. 19:27)

To help us understand the difference we have various terms. These show the different degrees of honor. In theology we distinguish between the Greek term *"doulia,"* which is the honor given to the saints, and the term *"hyperdulia"* which is the highest honor that can be given to a saint and is reserved for Mary. The term *"latria "* is the highest form of honor, glory, and praise which goes to the level of worship and thus is reserved for God alone. Worship is the highest, the ultimate form of honor, praise, and glory which is reserved for God alone. Worship involves an honor, praise, and glory that we give to God which is unlimited, complete, and total. So, this is the difference between the legitimate honor, praise, and glory given to men, and the worship that is for God alone. Christ honored men when he called John the Baptist greatest prophet (Lk. 7:28) and St. Peter blessed. (Mt. 16:17) He also said he would share His glory with his followers:

"I am praying for them; I am not praying for the world but for those whom thou hast given me, for they are thine; {10} all mine are thine, and thine are mine, and *I am glorified in them... {22} The glory which thou hast given me I have given to them,..."* (Jn. 17:9, 10, 22)

If he shares his glory with his followers, does not Mary receive the greatest share of glory? She was the most faithful disciple of Jesus, so He is glorified in her the most. So, as Jesus honored his followers of course He honored his mother, both on earth, and in heaven "...upon her head a crown of twelve stars." (Rev. 12:1) Jesus honors his Apostles: "And the wall of the city had twelve foundations, and on them the twelve names of the twelve apostles of the Lamb." (Rev. 21:14) On earth we are commanded to honor our parents in the 4th commandment, "Honor your father and mother."

On a spiritual level we worship our Father in heaven, and we honor our Immaculate Mother in heaven. So we see in scripture that holy men are honored, such as father Abraham, Moses, and Elijah. We even see that Abraham was a consolation to his fellow saints in the next world: "The poor man died and was carried by the angels to Abraham's bosom." (Lk. 16:22) Well Mary is "Blessed among all women" and she is blessed above all men, except for Jesus. Mary is placed in a special role in the kingdom of her son. He is the King; she is the Queen and Mother of the kingdom of God. So, of all the honor given to men, except Jesus, she is given the highest honor. She was the most faithful to God of all humans (except Jesus) who ever lived. She was the most faithful disciple of Jesus. Jesus kept the commandments by honoring his mother on earth. When Jesus dwells within us, his mystical body the church on earth, he continues to honor his mother through us. He not only honors his mother on earth, he honors her in heaven. She is the one he chose to be his mother before the world began, and she has replaced Eve as the spiritual mother of all the living. (Gen. 3:20, Rev. 12:17) Adam's and Eve's disobedience lost us paradise, the obedience of Mary (Lk. 1:38) initiates the process of salvation given by Jesus which restores us to paradise. We are commanded to honor our earthly parents in the fourth commandment, "Honor your father and mother." On a spiritual level we worship our Father in heaven, and we honor our Immaculate Mother in heaven. Our earthly parents represent our heavenly parents and prepare us to be with them together forever in heaven. After all God is the God of our Fathers, and our earthly fathers join us in praying, "Our Father who art in heaven..." Adam was the father of our fathers, but he was replaced by Christ, the "new Adam." (1Cor. 15:22) Mary is the spiritual Mother of our mothers, and they teach us to honor her who is our common Mother in the spiritual realm. Eve was the mother of all mothers, for she is the mother of all women on an earthly level. Mary is the New Eve, and she is "Blessed among all women" on a spiritual level. The role God chose for Mary began on earth, but was completed in heaven when he made his earthly mother his heavenly Queen. Christ is the son of David. Just as the earthly son of David, King Solomon, seated his Queen Mother Bathsheba at his side in his earthly court, so too does Christ the heavenly son of David, seat his Queen Mother at his right side in his heavenly court.

"{17} And he said, *'Pray ask* King Solomon—he will not refuse you—to give me Abishag the Shunammite as my wife.' {18} Bathsheba said, 'Very well; I will speak for you to the king.' {19} So Bathsheba went to King Solomon, to speak to him on behalf of Adonijah. And the king rose to meet her, and bowed down to her; then he sat on his throne, and had a seat brought for the king's mother; and she sat on his right. {20} Then she said, 'I have one small request to make of you; do not refuse me.' And the king said to her, *'Make your request, my mother; for I will not refuse you.'"* (1K. 2)

Part of the problem with Catholic devotion to Mary being so misunderstood centers around the understanding of the way Catholics use the term "pray." Notice how scripture says "pray ask" (1K. 2:17). So the connection between the words "pray" and "ask" is a logical and ancient one. When we honor Mary it is different from the worship we give to God. For some Protestants who oppose devotion to Mary they understand the term pray in a narrow exclusive way which means "worship only." When we "pray to God" we use this phrase in another sense, meaning worship with petition—or asking for help and favors. When we use the phrase, "Pray to Mary" it has a different meaning than the phrase, "Pray to God." When we pray to Mary, we are honoring her, we are asking for her help through her prayers, and we are enjoining her to join us in worship of God. So this phrase, "pray to Mary" which is often so misunderstood means, to pray to God, to honor Mary, to enjoin Mary in the Worship of God with us, and to request her prayers for us and with us. So there is worship involved when we pray to Mary, but it is the worship of God alone which accompanies the honor of Mary, and the worship of God is done by us along with Mary, our heavenly prayer partner.

Mary is honored by God the Father, God the Son, and God the Holy Spirit. Mary is honored by the Angels and the Saints. When we honor Mary, it pleases God, and he rewards us with graces and blessings. God chose to have his Son work his first miracle through her intercession and everyday all over the world God continues to work miracles and answer prayers, which come to him through her intercession. She is the beloved daughter of the Eternal Father, she is the Holy Mother of his only beloved Son, and she is the beautiful Bride of the Holy Spirit. Do we dare speak ill of her? Would God not punish us? Do we speak well of her, honor her, and love her? Would God not reward us for doing so? Are we not adopted sons in the family of God? Is she not the mother of the Son of God? When Christ dwells within us does she not become our spiritual mother? Is it not right for us as sons to honor and defend her? Did he not say to her she had a new relationship with his disciples at his death? Did he not say to her "Woman, behold your son."? (Jn. 19) Did he not say to all of his disciples who were represented by John at the foot of the cross, "Behold your mother."? (Jn. 19:27) Let us behold our spiritual Mother, and let us honor her with the word of God in the Hail Mary prayer. For the Hail Mary is a great gift which enables us to share in the mysterious love of God which he shows us through his mother. As scripture says,

"And a great sign appeared in heaven: a woman clothed with the sun, and the moon was under her feet, and upon her head a crown of twelve stars...And the dragon was angered at the woman, and went away to wage war with the rest of her offspring, who keep the commandments of God, and hold fast the testimony of Jesus."　(Rev. 12:1,17)

For we are the rest of her offspring, she is our mother, and the devil wages war against us. And, she is our loving mother who fights for us, and with us, against the dragon. She does this with her prayers for us, her beloved children. And, we obtain this help through the Hail Mary prayer.

Christ is our only mediator (1 Tim. 2:5-6) with the Father, but Mary can intercede (pray for us) with her Son Jesus. By very definition, angels are messengers of God. The words that the Archangel Gabriel used to speak to Mary do not come from him, but are a sacred message delivered to Mary from God the Father. The word "hail" is a word of honor. It is this word that the Eternal Father uses to honor the daughter he created to be the mother of his only beloved son. When we pray the Hail Mary we pray the word of God, and honor Mary as God the Father does, and it pleases him. He created these words specifically for her honor and to begin the new covenant, for they are the first words of the Gospel. It was these words which began the event of the incarnation which occurred at the annunciation. God the Father was the first to say these words of the Hail Mary prayer, and the Archangel Gabriel was the second. These are the words which began the salvation of the world, the Angelic Salutation, the words of honor sent from God the Father for the mother of his only beloved son. This is why we say them so much, for they are the cornerstone of the Gospel, they are the words which prepared Mary for the "Word" to be made flesh and dwell among us.

The second verse of the Hail Mary prayer comes from the Holy Spirit, and he is the first to say these words which are given to and spoken by St. Elizabeth. The Holy Spirit honors Mary by saying, "Blessed are you among women, and blessed is the fruit of your womb, Jesus." It is the word of God, and when we pray this prayer we pray the word of God, we join the Holy Spirit in Honoring Mary, his spouse. As scripture says:

"...that which is conceived in her is of the Holy Spirit."   (Mt. 1:20)

"And the Word became flesh and dwelt among us, full of grace..." (Jn. 1:14)

The Hail Mary is the result of the union of the Word of God in Sacred Scripture and Sacred Tradition. The last verse of the Hail Mary prayer is the result of the Sacred Tradition of the Church, and centuries of honoring Mary, of asking for her prayers, and the fruit of the Holy Spirit dwelling within the Saints of the Church. "Holy Mary, Mother of God, pray for us sinners, now and at the hour of our death." Amen.

Who can argue with the truths expressed in this prayer? Is Mary not Holy? Is she not full of grace? Is Mary not the Mother of God? Can she who is the Queen of Angels and Saints, and sits at the right hand of the Son of God in heaven not pray for us now and at the hour of our death? To argue against the Hail Mary is to argue against God. For the Hail Mary is the Word of God in prayer, and the words of the "Hail Mary" come from God. God said the first "Hail Mary" through the Archangel Gabriel, through the Mother of John the Baptist, and through the voice of His Church.

So, the bottom line question still burns on: Why honor Mary when we can worship God alone apart from her? For those who have experienced how devotion to Mary helps them love Jesus Christ and serve God better, a fuller explanation is not really necessary. They are living the answer which they know is true by experience. For they who have had their prayers answered through Mary have experienced that devotion and honor of Mary is a help given by God to assist us in loving God and our neighbor. For those who have not experienced the powerful spiritual love of Mary their heavenly Mother, an academic intellectual reason is still sought. I have a simple one to give. God has chosen to lead the way in the honor of Mary as an example for us to follow. He has said the first Hail Mary. For it was the word of God the Father that the archangel Gabriel delivered when he said those words which honor Mary. It was God the Father who began the salvation of the world with the word "Hail Mary, full of grace the Lord is with you." God began the Gospel with words of praise and honor for Mary, and the Holy Spirit followed up with "Blessed are you among women, and Blessed is the fruit of your womb Jesus." So it is God who first Honors Mary, he shows us the way. Can we err if we follow God? To properly honor Mary, that is to say because of her role as the supreme Mother and servant of God, is to also worship God. The proper honor of Mary *is* the worship of God, for the two are linked by the wisdom of God. The devil seeks to attack this mysterious union of God and Mary in the plan of salvation, to attack the New Eve as he did the first Eve. He seeks us to have the second death by separating us from Mary the New Eve, as he gave us the first death by bringing sin to the first Eve. He could not defeat the New Adam—Christ, or the New Eve—Mary, and when we unite our spirituality to Jesus and Mary he cannot defeat us. Let us not share in the defeat of Eve and believe the lies of the serpent, "Did God say..?" (Gen. 3:1) Let us share in the victory of the New Eve, and believe the word of God in Luke, "Hail Mary full of Grace the Lord is with you, blessed are you among women, and blessed is the fruit of your womb Jesus!"

Yes, God did say, "Hail Mary full of grace the Lord is with you..." and now when we pray this prayer we say it too! God tells the truth about Mary, and we benefit from this truth. She is His Mother, she is our Mother. He honors her and blesses her with many graces; we honor her and he blesses us with many graces.

The Rosary: The Heart of Devotion to Mary

"And Mary said, 'My soul magnifies the Lord ...For behold,
henceforth all generations will call me blessed; {49} for he who
is mighty has done great things for me, and holy is his name.'"
(Lk. 1:47, 48)

Mary's soul magnifies the Lord, and all generations will honor her with the title "Blessed." Scripture says that he who is mighty has done great things for her, what are those things? We are called by God to honor Mary as he did. In the early Church there was devotion to Mary. According to tradition the Angelic Salutation or Hail Mary was the earliest prayer to Mary. It comes straight from the scriptures. There were also other prayers as well. Before a thing is written it is usually said. We find one of the earliest written prayers to Mary found on an Egyptian papyrus written around 250 A.D. It is called the "Sub Tuum" in Latin, but it is originally written in Greek. An English translation reads:

"Beneath your compassion,
We take refuge, O Mother of God:
do not despise our petitions in time of trouble:
but rescue us from dangers, only pure, only blessed one."

70

The Hail Mary prayer is at the Heart of Devotion to Mary. Whatever other prayers there are to Mary, the Hail Mary has pre-eminence among all the prayers to Mary. God was the first one to pray the Hail Mary. God the Father gave the words, "Hail Mary full of grace the Lord is with thee" to the Archangel Gabriel. He came and repeated these words from heaven on the earth. It was with these words that God Honored Mary, then the Archangel Honored Mary, and now we Honor Mary with these words. God the Holy Spirit Honored Mary, through St. Elizabeth saying: "Blessed are you among women, and blessed is the fruit of your womb, Jesus."

The Hail Mary prayer is the core of the prayers of the Rosary, and it is often misunderstood. First of all we need to recognize that God Himself chose to unite the honor of Jesus with the honor of Mary. "Blessed are you among women, and blessed it the fruit of your womb Jesus." So, God has chosen for our salvation to unite the two together through the incarnation. Mary's role in the incarnation, being the Mother of God and the New Eve, is underestimated in value by those who reject devotion to Mary. God has rewarded her for her role as the New Eve, the Spouse of the Holy Spirit, the one who said, and "Let it be done to me according to your word."(Lk. 1:38)

The significance of this act for our salvation is great; this action of Mary represented mankind to God. Just as Eve's sin represented and affected us all for evil, so too did Mary's graceful consent (fiat) represent and affect us all for good. There were two major players in the beginning of sin for mankind, Adam and Eve. Likewise, there were two major figures in the end of sin and the beginning of grace. Adam's role was more significant than Eve's, but without Eve's consent Adam would not have sinned. The role of Jesus in redemption is more significant than Mary's, but without Mary's consent there would not have been an incarnation. Just as Eve's action had tremendous consequences for evil in the lives of us all, so too Mary's action had tremendous consequences for good in the lives of us all. God has chosen to reward her, to honor her for her role in his plan of salvation. Those who downgrade this role of Mary as the Mother of God and as our spiritual Mother attack the very foundations of the Gospel and risk their own damnation.

Of all human beings the role of Mary in the Gospel is the most significant. The connection between Mary and Jesus began at the incarnation/annunciation and continues forever. Her role is not diminished after the birth of Jesus. Her connection with her son is permanent on many levels, physically, spiritually, emotionally, and mystically. She is at the foot of the cross watching the body that he derived from hers die for the sins of the world. She more than anyone present knew who he was and what was happening. When she agreed to be the instrument of the incarnation, she also accepted all the consequences of that decision which included giving consent to offer her son in sacrifice on the cross and consent to become the mother of all his disciples. The world does not recognize its indebtedness to Mary. It does not recognize a just need for humanity to show her gratitude for what she has done for us. However God does recognize what she has done for us, and of her great sufferings. I believe Mary has suffered more than any other saint. Until we enter heaven itself mankind shall not fully comprehend the significance of the words of Mary at the Annunciation. Representing all of mankind, the whole human race, she said:

"And Mary said, 'Behold, I am the handmaid of the Lord; let it be to me according to your word.'" (Lk. 1:28)

Other than the words of Christ himself, no human ever spoke more significant words for humanity than Mary's words, "Let it be done to me according to your word…"

If I may digress for a moment I would like to look at a secular song which in an unusual way gives an indirect honor to the words of Mary. My intention here is not to "canonize" this secular song. I intend to use it as a springboard to jog our minds into a better understanding of the significance of Mary's words of consent. These words led to the Incarnation of Christ, which led to the redemption of the world. So these words began the Gospel, and Mary's acceptance of God's request represented us all. It was the first giant step on the stairway to heaven, the way back to Paradise. Her consent connected heaven to earth. It put God in man and reconnected man to God in a way unseen since it was severed by Adam and Eve. It was the reversal of Eve's consent to the forbidden fruit. This original sin is why we aren't in Paradise right now.

The Beatles song: *Let It Be* has a strange spiritual shadow to it that seems to point to these words of Mary. Paul McCartney's mother's name was Mary, and she was a Catholic. According to folklore the song is a reference to a dream he had during his anxiety about the bands imminent breakup. His mother appeared to him in the dream telling him to let it be, meaning to let what happens to the band not trouble him. The song ironically seems to have a spiritual side. The phrase "Mother Mary" is often used by devoted Catholics to apply to our spiritual mother Mary. The other phrase "hour of darkness" is used by Jesus in reference to the betrayal of Judas, and the sacrifice which led to the redemption of the world. People often use this phrase to refer to moments of great suffering and sacrifice in their lives. The "hour of darkness" (Lk. 22:53) is when things seem to be the worst, and we turn to God for help. In this song, there is a reference to the help of "mother Mary" and her presence "standing right in front of me." The song begins:

"When I find myself in times of trouble, mother Mary comes to me, speaking words of wisdom, let it be. And in my hour of darkness she is standing right in front of me, speaking words of wisdom, let it be."

As Catholics we also believe that she is present to pray for us when we ask for her prayers. We, who are devoted to Mary, often pray in Church or at home, with a statue of Mary standing right in front of us. The statue is a symbol of her spiritual presence for her spiritual children. Catholics often pray the Hail Mary in their time of need, and find comfort in the presence of Mary and her prayers. The whispered words of wisdom uttered by "mother Mary" are strangely enough, "Let it be." These are the words in fact uttered by Mother Mary at the annunciation to the angel. Mary's words, "Let it be," began the redemption of the world. The phrase, "there will be an answer let it be," can easily be interpreted in a spiritual way [though probably not intended!] to point to the answer God gives to Mary for her consent. The answer to Mary and to all of us is: "Jesus." He is our only hope of peace in this world and the next. At the resurrection of the dead we will "wake up to the sound of music" when the angel blows the trumpet:

"...with the sound of the trumpet of God... the dead in Christ will rise first." (1Thess. 4:16) The song says:

"I wake up to the sound of music, mother Mary comes to me, speaking words of wisdom, let it be."

The song speaks of a "light that shines on me," and we consider Christ to be "the light of the world." Scripture says: "I am the light of the world..." (Jn. 8:12) "The light shines in the darkness, and darkness grasped it not." (Jn. 1:5) The light that shines at night is the moon and it reflects the light of the sun as Mary reflects the light of her Son. Scripture uses the moon as a symbol for the feminine. (Gen. 37:9, 10) Intentionally or not, the song seems to touch on this theme:

"And when the night is cloudy, there is still a light that shines on me, shine until tomorrow, let it be."

When mother Mary wisely says: "Let it be" to God's request, the savior arrives who is the answer to all our prayers. The phrase, "Let it be" uttered by Mary the Mother of God is a phrase of acceptance and submission to God's will. Her acceptance of God's will leads to the arrival of God on earth! So there is wisdom in the acceptance of God's will and it leads to the answer to all of life's questions and desires. The simple phrase, "Let it be" spoken by Mary to the Archangel Gabriel led to the acceptance of Christ into the human family. Our acceptance of God's will brings us into the family of God. So these simple words were the most significant words which began the new world of grace and light, in this old world of darkness and sin. In the beginning of the world God said, "let there be light..." (Gen. 1) and then he created man and woman. In the beginning of the new world God created the woman who would answer God's request to bear his Son, and Mary said: "Let it be done unto me according to your word." (Lk. 1) So this song repeats these words on one level, but their significance can be lifted to another:

"Let it be, let it be, let it be, let it be. Whisper words of wisdom, let it be. And when the broken-hearted people living in the world agree, there will be an answer, let it be. For though they may be parted there is still a chance that they will see, there will be an answer. Let it be."

When we understand the full significance of Mary's words then we will understand her role in the saving of the world from sin. God recognizes it, and he has placed her name above every other human name except that of Jesus.

These words of consent did not just mean great joy, but also meant great suffering for her. The silent suffering of Mary is shown by the sword piercing her immaculate heart. What does the world know of the suffering of Mary? I believe the humility and suffering of Mary to be the greatest of all the saints. The scriptures themselves make several references to her suffering, starting with the reference to the "sword" that will pierce her heart and soul (Lk. 2:35) and her mystical birth pangs at the foot of the cross. (Jn. 19:26, 27, Rev.12:2) When does this sword pierce her heart? At the foot of the cross Mary watches the lance go through the side of Christ, and the sword of sorrow pierces her heart. The external suffering of Jesus is felt in perfect empathy in the sinless immaculate Heart of Mary. This is a great mystery we will only understand when we have entered heaven.

The role of Mary as the New Eve is a major key for understanding the role of Mary. The Incarnation is another major key for understanding the role of Mary in salvation and in our spirituality. Just as a Mother has a permanent connection with her son in life, so too does Mary have a permanent connection with Jesus. Many times in an attempt to downplay Mary's role in salvation it is argued that it was Jesus who was crucified not Mary, and this is true. However, this perspective misses a certain theological importance of the incarnation. Without the incarnation there was no passion, death, and resurrection, and without Mary there was no incarnation.

Mary is the person created by God specifically for this role, and so she is set apart from all of humanity for a special place. She is first among all the Saints, the first to give her life to Christ. She is also the one whose decision to say "yes" resulted in her giving life to Christ as a mother. She was the instrument through which Christ entered into our human family. As part of that role he has chosen her to be the spiritual Mother of the family of God. As a mother is connected with bearing and raising her son, so too is Mary connected with the work of her son. How can this be? Every mother is connected with the work of her son because it is through the mother that there is a son. A mother shares in the work of her son because she provided the presence of the son which is the foundation for all the work of the son. So, all the work of Christ as our redeemer is connected to the work of Mary as his Mother. Mary's work as Mother was the Incarnation of God. The Incarnation was the first step towards the redemption of the world. We see in the Gospel that the Angel is informing Mary of the greatness of her future son, and confirming her "favor with God." He is also telling her to name him "Jesus," and that he will be "called holy, the Son of God." So, Mary accepts the call of God to be his mother, and the lives of Jesus and Mary are tied together forever. Scripture says:

"In the beginning was the Word... and the Word was God...and the word became flesh and dwelt among us." (Jn. 1) Do not be afraid, Mary, **for you have found favor with God. {31} And behold, you will conceive in your womb and bear a son, and you shall call his name Jesus. {32} He will be great, and will be called the Son of the Most High; and the Lord God will give to him the throne of his father David, {33} and he will reign over the house of Jacob for ever; and of his kingdom there will be no end."** {34} And Mary said to the angel, 'How shall this be, since I have no husband?' {35} And the angel said to her, 'The Holy Spirit will come upon you, and the power of the Most High will overshadow you; therefore the child to be born will be called holy, the Son of God.'" (Lk. 1:30-35)

God commands us to honor our mothers because they worked with God to bring about our beginning. As God, Jesus has no beginning, but as man he does. Although Jesus existed before Mary, she was chosen to be the instrument of the incarnation, the beginning of Jesus as a man. She was the instrument of the incarnation and God honors her and rewards her for that role in redemption. Are we not intimately connected to our parents? Are we not the result of the union of our Father and Mother? Mary conceived by the Holy Spirit, and so her relationship with the Holy Trinity is more intimate, more unique, and more significant than another other human being. I believe there is a certain hidden spiritual envy of those who seek to downplay the role of Mary. I think those hearts are too spiritually proud to admit that there is someone so much more significant than they are in the family of God. A son is blessed by God for honoring his Father and Mother. Christ is the Son of Mary, and he honors her perfectly as God and man. He honors her in this world and in the next, as a Son during his life on earth, and in his mystical body the church. So, Christ the son continues to honor his Father and mother through his mystical body the church. The connection that began at the incarnation continues forever, and she is spiritually and mystically united with all the work of Christ in the Gospel. The foundation of the presence of Christ on earth is the Incarnation, and the foundation of the incarnation is Mary. God does not downplay the free will or work of Mary in the incarnation, so neither should we. Humanity is indebted to Mary for her role in the incarnation. Humanity is commanded by God to express its gratitude to her through honoring her. Our indebtedness and gratitude to Mary are expressed in the Hail Mary prayer, which comes from God. Those who do not understand the Gospel seek to minimize the role of Mary, and deny the honor that is due to her by humanity. God understands the Gospel and He gives us the words to honor her as he has honored her.

Part of the problem is the worldliness of man always links power with pride. It is not so in heaven. Jesus says:

"But Jesus called them to him and said, 'You know that the rulers of the Gentiles lord it over them, and their great men exercise authority over them. {26} It shall not be so among you; but whoever would be great among you must be your servant, {27} and whoever would be first among you must be your slave; {28} even as the Son of man came not to be served but to serve, and to give his life as a ransom for many.'" (Mt. 20:25-28)

Mary is the humble servant of the Lord and of all of mankind. She agreed to be the vehicle of the incarnation and all the sacrifices, sorrows, and sufferings it entailed. She gave her all for God and man. Mary was born humble, she lived humbly, and as Queen of Heaven and earth she reigns in humility. Scripture says:

"And Mary said, 'My soul magnifies the Lord, {47} and my spirit rejoices in God my Savior, for *he has regarded the low estate of his handmaiden.* For behold, henceforth all generations will call me blessed; {49} for he who is mighty has done great things for me, and holy is his name. {50} And his mercy is on those who fear him from generation to generation. {51} He has shown strength with his arm, *he has scattered the proud in the imagination of their hearts,* {52} *he has put down the mighty from their thrones, and exalted those of low degree...*" (Lk. 1:47-52)

We may hear it said, "why are there ten Hail Mary prayers in the Rosary instead of ten Our Fathers?" The answer is very simple; because God has chosen to involve Mary in our salvation as our principal representative after Jesus. Jesus is God and man, but Mary is human only. She is not divine. God has given her a role in salvation that is the most significant after Jesus. In God's plan, it is Mary that agrees to become the Mother of God, and she says yes to Jesus for all of us. Her "yes" begins salvation. Her "yes" changes the world. Her "yes" gives Jesus to the world. She says "yes" to Jesus for the first time and her "yes" is the most significant of all the saints who said "yes" to Jesus. So, in the prayer God himself commands the Angel, who is only a messenger of God, to say:

"Hail Mary full of grace the Lord is with thee." (Lk. 1:28)

So, in the first line we see God honors Mary with the word "hail" **and the name of the Lord is mentioned and honored as well**. The honor of Mary is based on what? It is based on the fact that: "the Lord is with thee." So, she is being blessed for being with the Lord. So is the Hail Mary prayer all about Mary and not about God? How absurd! The Hail Mary is the word of God, and God does not dishonor himself! So the ten Hail Marys are about Honoring Mary in her relationship to God and his Son. It is also honoring her in her role as our spiritual mother and asking for her prayers for "us sinners" since she is without sin. She is the New Eve, the New Sinless Virgin created by God who is victorious over the ancient serpent the devil. So, the serpent works very hard to deceive us about her role in God's plan for our salvation. She is our praying spiritual Mother, who prays more for us as we honor her more. This is a matter of great concern for the serpent, for God said, "I will put enmity between you and the woman...." (Gen. 3:15)

Let us look at the next line and see how false the argument against the Hail Mary is:

"Blessed are you among women, and blessed is the fruit of your womb, Jesus."

It is strange for a prayer that supposedly steals honor away from Jesus and erroneously gives it to Mary to say, "**Blessed is... Jesus.**" So we see the fact is that every Hail Mary prayer blesses Jesus as well as mentions and honors "the Lord." It looks like there is a problem for those who forget to look at the words and argue against the ten Hail Marys in the Rosary as a way Jesus is honored less. Let us look at the final line and see what the words show us:

"Holy Mary, Mother of God, pray for us sinners, now and at the hour of our death."

So Mary is obviously Holy, as she is blessed among all women and men except Jesus. The name of God is mentioned again, in his relationship to Mary. So "God" is not forgotten but is mentioned. So honor is not stolen from God in the Hail Mary. The difference is God is honored through Mary, as he Himself has chosen. Who seeks to destroy this union of God and Mary, in prayer and in Honor? It is not God, for he has ordained it to be so. It is the enemy of God and man, the ancient serpent who attacked the first sinless virgin in paradise with his false words that led to sin. Now, he is continuing his lying words attacking the New Eve with his false words that lead us to the sin of dishonoring Mary and depriving us of the power of her prayers to help us escape from the serpent.

"Then the dragon was angry with the woman, and went off to make war on the rest of her offspring, on those who keep the commandments of God and bear testimony to Jesus." (Rev. 12:17)

So, in the Hail Mary prayer, which is falsely accused of neglecting or stealing honor from God, we find the following. Mary is only honored in her relationship with God, only honored because she loves God as God wishes us to do. The word Mary is mentioned twice, but only in her subordinate relationship to God. And, her honor is due only because of her closeness to God. We find also the words "Lord," "Jesus," and

"God" in the Hail Mary prayer. So, in the Hail Mary prayer we honor the "Lord," we honor "Jesus," and we honor "God." Every time we pray the "Hail Mary," we are also praying in worship and honor of "the Lord," of "Jesus," and of "God." So we are worshipping God with Mary when we say this prayer. For we worship God for what he has done for us through Mary when we say this prayer. For in the Hail Mary prayer, we find "The Lord," "Jesus," "God," "Mary," "grace," "blessed," "pray" and "us sinners" all come together in one beautiful prayer given by God himself.

The prayer is a foundational reminder of the goodness of "God" and the goodness of being with "the Lord" and his "grace." When we honor Mary with the words, "the Lord is with you," we are witnessing to the goodness of the Lord for her and for us. When we honor Mary with the words "full of grace" we are witnessing to the goodness of God's grace for her and for us. We see what he has done for Mary, through Mary, and with Mary, for us sinners. Jesus has chosen to come to us on earth "through Mary," and so she is intimately united to the mission of the incarnation and the redemption of the world. So, Jesus has also chosen to have Mary help us come to him through her prayers, which are the most powerful of all his Saints. Every time we pray the Hail Mary prayer, she prays for us and with us, to help "us sinners" get to heaven. The idea that this prayer is all about Mary and not about God is a total distortion of the words and the meaning of this prayer. The idea that this prayer takes honor due to God, or takes honor from God, and gives it to Mary is absurd. The prayer is all about God's goodness, God's grace, and God's presence, and God's love that come to us through Mary. God's goodness, grace, and presence come to us through Jesus, first at the incarnation and now through her prayers to him on our behalf.

The idea that the role of Mary in the incarnation is somehow insignificant, irrelevant or a minor action on her part is a false understanding of the event. Jesus "chose" her as his mother and as our mother. She is significant to Him and to us. He has chosen to magnify her soul, to make her "blessed among all women," and for her to be held in the highest honor in heaven and on earth. It is a grave error for a Christian to believe the role of Mary in the Gospel and in the plan of salvation is insignificant, irrelevant, or minor. God has chosen to give humble Mary a significant, relevant, and major role in the Gospel and in the plan of salvation. This prayer is "the prayer" from God that brings the family of God, Mary, us sinners, and Jesus together. This prayer is the cornerstone of the reason the Son of God appeared to destroy the works of the devil. The Gospel, that touches upon the role of Mary at the Incarnation of Christ, and the role of Mary as our spiritual Mother who prays for us in heaven.

Also, in this prayer we humble ourselves by recognizing we are sinners. So it is a prayer of humility, "pray for us sinners." It is also absurd to argue that we are "worshipping Mary in the Hail Mary prayer." The words themselves say, "Mother of God, pray for us...." How odd that a prayer that is falsely accused of "worshipping Mary," should request her prayers to God for us! If we were treating her as God we wouldn't be asking for her to pray to God for us!!! In the Hail Mary prayer she prays to God and we pray to God. In the Hail Mary prayer you have the highest saint in heaven, the one who is without sin, praying for us "sinners" to help us get to heaven. We are obtaining great graces from God each time we pray this prayer which we could not obtain any other way. So the idea that the Hail Mary competes with the Our Father is an absurdity. The Hail Mary complements the Our Father, and works with the Our Father prayer to give true worship and honor to God. The difference is that the Hail Mary prayer shows recognition for the role that the woman God chose to be his Mother and our Mother. This is within the context of the Gospel, because the arrival of Christ begins with the incarnation in the womb of Mary. So, the Hail Mary is the worship of God in relation to that person, Mary, through whom the incarnation arose. God does not neglect her honor, and if we are smart we won't either. She is a spiritual gift, a spiritual "helpmate" from God to help make the road of the cross to heaven, an easier, safer, and shorter route. For God said, "it is not good for the man to be alone; I will make him a helpmate." (Gen. 2:18) "Behold your mother." (Jn. 19) So, we are not alone, we have Mary. Mary is the helpmate of the Church, the Family of God, and the Mystical body of Christ. Jesus is our savior, and he is God become Man. Mary is only human, but she is the gate through which God became man.

"Then the Lord God said, "It is not good that the man should be alone; I will make him a helper fit for him." (Gen. 2:18)

Mary is our helper that is fit for us, for she is without sin, she is the perfect disciple; she is the way that God chose to become one of us. She is the way that God chose to help us more than any other human besides Jesus, to help us follow him.

When we consider these facts the idea that the ten Hail Marys in the Rosary steal honor from God becomes absurd. The Rosary contains the prayers of the Our Father, Hail Mary, and Glory Be, prayed in conjunction with the meditation on the Gospel. The Rosary is the meditation on the life of Jesus, which began in Mary at the Annunciation, and continues through the passion, death, and resurrection. These meditations end with Jesus crowning Mary Queen of Heaven and Earth showing recognition for the one he chose to be his mother and our mother. Do we dare neglect to honor her whom he has so honored? God has chosen to honor her—do we join Him or oppose him?

The Rosary is the prayer in the center of the Immaculate Heart of Mary. It is this prayer she requested so many times in her early visits in places like Lourdes and Fatima. "Pray the rosary daily," could be said to be the central message of all Marian apparitions. Sister Lucia is one of the few people who actually spoke with the Blessed Virgin Mary. Her words are very important in helping us to understand the role of Mary in our spiritual lives. It is important to note that Pope Benedict XVI has lifted the five-year waiting period to start the canonization process for Carmelite Sister Lucia dos Santos. She is one of the three children who saw Our Lady of Fatima in 1917. In commenting on the Hail Mary and the Rosary, Sister Lucia of the Fatima Apparition said:

"'Hail, full of grace, the Lord is with you!' (Lk. 1:26-28) I think that when He was sending the Angel, God must have suggested to him the words with which he was to salute Mary, announcing to her, on the part of God, the mystery of the incarnation of the Word. And St. Elizabeth, moved by the Holy Spirit, said: 'Blessed are you among women, and blessed is the fruit of your womb!' (Lk. 1, 42) Thus, the Hail Mary was formed under God's inspiration... **We must regard this salutation as having been addressed to the Virgin Mary by God himself...** If St.

Elizabeth was moved by the Holy Spirit when she uttered these words, as Sacred Scripture tells us; then this praise comes from the Holy Spirit. But it is more praise of God than of Mary: You are blessed because the fruit of your womb is blessed; and it is in this fruit, and by this fruit, that the blessings of God have come to you and that you are blessed among all women. And this was how the Virgin Mary understood it when she sang: 'My soul magnifies the Lord...' (Lk. 1, 46-50) ...As we see all praise of Mary rises up to God; He looked with mercy on his lowly handmaid. So the Ave Maria is indeed a biblical prayer. But it is also part of the Liturgy, being recited on various feasts of the year, both in the Mass and in the Liturgy of the Hours. Later on, the Church, guided by the Holy Spirit Who enlightens and helps it, rounded off the formula of the Ave Maria with the humble supplication: "Holy Mary, Mother of God, pray for us sinners, now and at the hour of our death. Amen." There is, thus, only one divine Mediator: Jesus Christ; but as supplicant intercessors we have Mary, the saints, and each one of us, if we so wish. St. Paul himself, in various passages in his letters, asks people to pray both for him and for one another. 'To that end keep alert with all perseverance, making supplication for all the saints, and also for me.' (Eph. 6, 18-20) So, if the Apostle tells us to pray for one another, we have much more reason to ask Mary to pray for us, because her prayer will be much more pleasing to the Lord in view of her dignity as Mother of God and her closer union with Christ, true God and true Man, by reason of her mission of co-Redemptrix with Christ as well as of her great sanctity... Pope Pius IX... on his deathbed, he said to those around him: 'The Rosary is a compendium of the Gospel, and gives to those who pray it those rivers of peace of which the Scriptures speak; it is the most beautiful devotion, the most abundant in grace, and the most pleasing to the Heart of Mary. My sons, let this be the testimony by which you remember me on earth.' [February 1818]... There are those who say that the Rosary is an antiquated and monotonous prayer, because of the constant repetition of the prayers which compose it. But I put the question: Is there anything at all which lives except through the continual repetition of the same actions? Thus, in order to preserve our life, we breathe in and breathe out always in the same way; our heart beats all the time according to the same rhythm. The stars, the sun, the moon, the planets, the earth follow always the same course, which God has laid down for them. Day follows night, year after year, always in the same way. Likewise the sun gives us light and warmth. In so many plants the leaves appear in the spring, then they are clothed with flowers, next they yield fruit and, in autumn or winter, they lose their leaves. Thus, everything follows the law which God has laid down for it, and yet it never occurs to anyone to say that it is monotonous; hence, nobody says so; the fact is that we need all this in order to live! Well then! In the spiritual life we experience the same need to repeat continually the same prayers, the same acts of faith, hope and charity, in order to live, since our life is a continued participation in the life of God... ("Calls" From the Message of Fatima, by Sister Lucia, copyright Coimbra Carmel & Fatima Shrine, English translation by Sisters of Mosteiro de Santa Maria and Convento de N.S. do Bom Sucesso, Lisbon, pp. 264, 265, 266, 267, 271)

It is an absurd and misleading argument that says, "It's just me and Jesus in the universe and everything that is not Jesus blocks me from Jesus." This argument that anything that is not Jesus blocks us from Jesus is a lie from the devil designed to keep us away from the help that God has given us. We are part of a human family and a spiritual family, with God and our neighbor. God has chosen to use others to help us love him and help us serve him. When we honor our earthly mothers, we are serving God, loving God and God is pleased and blesses us with graces. When we honor our heavenly Mother (who is also the Mother of God the Son, the Daughter of the Father, and the Spouse of the Holy Spirit) we are serving God, loving God, and God is pleased and blesses us with graces. God uses persons, places and things, to help us love him. The scripture, pictures of Jesus, etc. are all things which help us love Jesus. Mary is our spiritual mother. Our family and our friends are sources of God's love by their words and examples and they all help us love Jesus. The idea that Mary, or the scripture, or our family and friends that teach us about God by their words and examples block us from loving Jesus is absurd. We imitate Christ who honored his mother.

Some have argued against devotion to Mary saying, "Only me and Jesus, nothing or no one else." But they forget the reality of God's methods. Persons, places, and things can and do help us get closer to Christ. A person who prays with us or for us, or teaches us the faith helps us get closer to Christ. A place such as a church or things such as a bible or crucifix can help us get closer to Christ. Christ uses persons, places, and things to help us on the road to salvation. Those who complain about Mary being in the way of coming to Christ need to remember that Christ uses persons, places, and things to help us get closer to Him.

Chapter 7

Mary is Our Spiritual Mother

"'Woman, behold your son!' Then he said to the disciple, 'Behold, your mother!'" (Jn. 19:27)

Mary is our Mother in the Family of God

Mary is the Queen Mother who is seated next to her son Jesus, in his glorious kingdom. As Queen Mother Bathsheba was next to her son Solomon, the son of David who prefigured or was a type of Christ. The advantage of asking a favor of the king through the queen's intercession was that the request is now linked to her and so has the power of her request, not only that of ours. So we see at the wedding of Cana that Mary's request is granted because of our Lord's love for his Mother. It says in Genesis "Eve became the mother of all the living." We understand Christ as the new Adam, and Mary as the new Eve. When we enter into the new covenant with Christ, we become part of his family. Mary is his mother, Mary is our mother. God the Father is his Father, God the Father is now our Father who art in heaven. Mary is our Mother, blessed among all women and full of grace.

When Jesus said to John "Behold your mother," and to Mary "Woman behold your son," it was not some poetic way of saying, "Take care of my mother after I'm gone." To dismiss the deeper meaning of these words of our Lord from the cross to his mother and his disciple is to try to deny the obvious. Unfortunately there are still many who will argue, when Jesus said these words, he didn't mean them. The truth is when he said, "Behold your mother" he meant she is now your mother in the kingdom of God. When he said to Mary, "Woman, behold your son" he meant to tell her she has now gained his disciples as her children, in addition to him. We know this from the meaning of the words "mother" and "son." St. John and the Virgin Mary are not blood relatives. He is not her physical son, and she is not his physical mother. Yet, Jesus now informs them that they are mother and son! So how are they mother and son if they are not according to the flesh? It can only be according to the spirit! So, if John is the son of Mary, and Mary is the Mother of John because he is a disciple of Jesus, then we are as well! For we are disciples of Christ, and Christ dwells within us. She is our mother and we are her sons!

When Jesus says to Mary "Behold your son," he does not mean John replaces him as her son. He is not denying that she still is his mother. However, his point is she is the mother of all his disciples in addition to being his mother. Notice that Jesus does not say to John, "Son, behold your mother." Jesus is our brother, a fellow son of Mary. We have the same Father—God. Jesus says with us "Our Father who art in heaven," and he chose Mary to be his mother and our mother. When Mary gave birth to Jesus, this birth is also linked to the church. Christ is the head of the church, and the church is the body of Christ. (Eph. 5:23-33, Col. 1:18) So could she give birth to the head and not to the body? Certainly not! Mary is the mother of Christ and the mother of the Church. She gave birth to Christ the head of the Church and to the Church as well, which is the mystical body of Christ. So the birth of Christ and the pain and sorrow she endured at the foot of the cross are spiritually united. It was at the end of Christ's life, with his last words from the cross, that he proclaimed Mary to be the mother of his disciples. She is proclaimed to be the mother of all the saved. The time and place of these words is significant, because the foot of the cross is the birth of the atonement for all sin which began at the tree of knowledge of good and evil. Jesus gives his mother to us at the moment he is redeeming the world. At the tree of the cross the new Eve, the mother of all the living in Christ, is given the second part of her mission. The first part of her mission was to be the Mother of God, and this was achieved at the nativity. Her mission as the New Eve was now taking the next step towards its completion as the Mother of the Church, the mother of all the saved. As a mother her job was to protect and nurture her children, she would do this through her sufferings on earth and in her prayers in heaven. Mary's contemplation of the passion of Christ was more perfect than any other human being. Her sorrow at the cross was the most perfect of any saint in heaven. Her love of her son was more total than any other human being, and Our Lord was to reward her with all the saints as her spiritual children. She was now the mother to the largest family in heaven and on earth—the Church.

Yet, there is more to this mysterious event at the cross of Calvary which reverses what happened at the tree of knowledge of good and evil. It was at the tree that Eve received the notice of punishment of pain in childbirth, and it was at the tree that Mary the new Eve, was notified of her deeper mission beyond that of being the mother of Jesus. It is here that Jesus says, "Behold," and announces to her and to John the words "Mother" and "Son," notifying each of their new spiritual relationship. The Archangel Gabriel announces to Mary that she will have a son named Jesus. Her son Jesus announces to her at the cross that she will have more sons, and St. John is the first of her new children to know. The new Adam is a son, and the new Eve is his mother, and the reversal of sin occurs when the grace of justification is merited for us on the cross. "Then as one man's trespass led to condemnation for all men, so one man's act of righteousness leads to acquittal and life for all men. {19} For as by one man's disobedience many were made sinners, so by one man's obedience many will be made righteous." (Rom. 5:18, 19) So the human family has a new Adam and a new Eve, and they are born into the new family of God through Holy Baptism. The family of God is to be fed the bread of life from the tree of the cross in the Holy Eucharist. It is here alone the Gospels record Jesus using the word, "Paradise," a word for the Garden of Eden or the Garden of Paradise. It is ironic that Jesus would use the word paradise from the cross, but that reminds us that he is opening the gate to paradise for us through his sufferings on the tree of the cross.

Why do we love our earthly mothers so much, and why does God command us to honor and love them so much? Do they do something to deserve this honor and love? Yes, our mothers give their lives for us not only in the pain of birthing us, but in the time and service they give to raising us from little babies to grown men. So in the natural order we defend our mother's honor, even to the point of battle on the school playground when bullies make sport of our mother's name. We also defend our spiritual mother against heretical bullies who would attack her role and honor in God's plan of salvation in the theological schoolyard of debate. Let us defend the Mother of God, let us defend our Mother! We know how much our mothers give to us and it is truly among the greatest sacrificial loves there are in life. The love of a mother for her son is powerful indeed. So then, how is this kind of sacrifice and love present in the life of Mary for her son Jesus and for her adopted spiritual sons like St. John the Apostle? In the book of Revelation we see St. John write of Mary in a mystical spiritual way. There is a strange time compression of events and interplay between heaven and earth, time and events. So the chronology and the symbolism in this chapter are difficult to interpret. We see the life of Jesus goes from his birth to his ascension into heaven, in Revelation chapter 12. And we see Mary being described in a glorified state even before his birth, "Clothed with the sun, and with a crown of twelve stars. But it says she "Wailed aloud as she gave birth." Remember Adam's punishment was death and earning his bread by the sweat of his brow. (Gen. 3:19) This is fulfilled by Jesus who sweat blood in the agony in the garden (Lk. 22:43) after giving us the bread of life at the last supper, the first Mass. Yet Jesus did not have his own sins to suffer for, he was a man without sin who suffered for our sins. Mary is the new Eve, like Eve at the tree of knowledge she too is without sin, yet she would suffer because of our sins at the tree of the cross. When would Mary "wail aloud as she gave birth" taking on the punishment of Eve for sin (Gen. 3:16) while she herself was without sin? At the foot of the cross Mary watched her son die a slow torturous death. She watched this horror with the innocence of a little child, yet she was an adult without sin. She did not eat the forbidden fruit of sin as we do. There is no doubt "Our Lady of Sorrows" earned her title that day at the foot of the cross, and "wailed aloud in pain" as she watched her Son die for our sins. She suffered for love of her Son Jesus Christ during that time more than any other saint ever suffered for sin. Only in heaven will we begin to understand the mystery of suffering that Christ allowed his mother on that day, and every day that she recalled his passion and death. This is what we do in the Rosary, we try to approximate the meditation, contemplation, and the empathy that Mary had for the suffering of Jesus at the foot of the cross when we meditate on the sorrowful mysteries. So did Mary's sufferings redeem us from sin? Certainly not! Did Mary's sufferings in some way help us in our salvation. They certainly did!

God chose this suffering for Mary as part of his plan for his Church, just as he chooses sufferings for us as part of his plan for our salvation. To St. Paul he said, "I will show him how much he must suffer for my name" (Acts 6:16), and St. Paul said, "Now I rejoice in my sufferings for your sake, and in my flesh I complete what is lacking in Christ's afflictions for the sake of his body, that is, the church." (Col. 1:24) What is lacking to the sufferings of Christ? Nothing is lacking to them, but their application to our soul. And, their continuous union to our soul involves us carrying our cross. "And he said to all, 'If any man would come after me, let him deny himself and take up his cross daily and follow me.'" (Lk. 9:23)

In the process of salvation Christ calls us to join our sufferings to His, and when they are united to His sufferings he gives them merit. In this way the grace of God works through man, and man is made to be like God when God lives and works in him. "Be imitators of Christ" for it is no longer I who live but Christ who lives in me. "The love with which thou hast loved me may be in them, and I in them." (Jn. 17:26) "Now I rejoice in my sufferings for your sake, and in my flesh I complete what is lacking in Christ's afflictions for the sake of his body, that is, the church," (Col. 1:24) says St. Paul. If this is true of the sufferings of saints like Paul, who had repented from persecuting Christians, what was the value of the sufferings of Mary who was without sin, and gave birth to God the Son for our salvation? What was the sorrowful cross of Mary that day as she, along with God the Father, watched her only beloved Son be scourged at the pillar, carry his cross, and be crucified! I would say she "wailed aloud in pain" as she gave birth to her new child, the church, and the church is the mystical "body of Christ." St. John the Apostle represented the whole church that day. Next to Mary at the foot of the cross, he represented all the disciples of Jesus in two ways. First, he was the only one of the twelve apostles, who was at the foot of the cross that day. The others had fled and did not return to Jesus as he had. Second, he was told to "Behold his mother" because as a son like Jesus in the family of God he would now have Mary as his mother. Jesus said to her, "Woman, behold your son." In the midst of her deep profound sorrows "she wailed aloud in pain" as she watched her son die on the cross, and Jesus gave her a new mission as the mother of all his disciples. Eve was the first "mother of all the living" and she failed by sinning. Mary succeeded because she did not sin, and at the foot of the cross she became the spiritual mother of all the living in Christ. (Rev. 12:17) So Mary's sorrow and suffering for her only beloved son Jesus, and for her many sons who became hers on that day, made her a mother who gave all for her children. We owe her a great debt as our spiritual mother, just as we owe a great debt to our earthly mother. So when we honor her with the word of God in the Hail Mary Prayer we pray, "Hail Mary full of grace the Lord is with thee." In this prayer we join God the Father in praising her; we join her Spouse the Holy Spirit in honoring and glorifying her who is "Blessed among all women." We thank her for giving birth to Jesus, we thank her for being at the foot of the cross, and we thank her for her love of Jesus and her love of us. We thank her for suffering so much at the foot of the cross for our sins, when she herself had no sin. She was to understand and know sin, by watching its effects of pain and death on the face of her only beloved son.

She is the suffering Mother of Jesus, and she is our suffering Mother who is saddened by our sins on earth. When we honor, praise, and glorify Mary for her love of God and neighbor, God is pleased and rewards us with graces and blessings. For when we honor her who loved him so much, he is pleased because he loved her so much, and he blesses us because he loves us so much. So there is a basic understanding of so great a mystery of how Mary has loved us so much and why God has called us to in turn love her so much.

On the cross, Christ was completing the heart of his mission on earth. The most difficult part of the redemption was the crucifixion. This is the mission for which he was born and the one that his mother enabled him to do at the annunciation. The same disciple who wrote these lines, "Behold your mother," in the Gospel of John, also wrote these lines in the book of Revelation: "The devil went off to make war against the rest of her children, those who keep the commandments of God and give witness to Jesus." (Rev. 12:17) Also notice Jesus does not say, "Son, behold your mother." For John has joined Jesus in the family of God. John has become a son of God who has God the Father as his father, and Mary as his mother. When God the son, joined the family of man, we humans also joined the family of God. It was a complete joining of families. The family of God joins the family of man, and the family of man joins the family of God.

The Trinity integrated into humanity at the incarnation and humanity integrates into the Trinity at baptism. "Baptize all nations in the name of the Father, and of the Son, and of the Holy Spirit...." (Mt. 28) We enter into the Divine Family of the Trinity, and we have God as our Father, Jesus as our brother, and the Holy Spirit dwelling within us. When Jesus enters into the human family he has Mary as his mother, and the rest of humanity as his brothers and sisters. Mary was chosen for this role because she did the will better than anyone else. It is important to keep that in mind when we read what our Lord says about membership in his family:

"Who are my mother and my brethren?' {34} And looking around on those who sat about him, he said, 'Here are my mother and my brethren! {35} Whoever does the will of God is my brother, and sister, and mother.'" (Mk. 5:33-35)

Jesus refers to the crowd around him as his mother and brothers to make a point that entrance into the family of God is not based on blood, but on grace. As scripture says:

"But to all who received him, who believed in his name, he gave power to become children of God; {13} who were born, not of blood nor of the will of the flesh nor of the will of man, but of God." (Jn. 1:13)

He does not mean to diminish the role of Mary in the kingdom of God. He is making another point. Mary's role in the kingdom is not based on unfair favoritism based on a blood relationship, but on a just role assigned to her by God based on a faith relationship wherein her obedience was the greatest. So, when we consider the point Jesus makes in this verse it still leads us back to Mary for she does the will of God more than any other member of the family of God. Jesus rejected the favoritism sought by the Jews based on their claims to blood relations, "...do not begin to say to yourselves, 'We have Abraham as our father'; for I tell you, God is able from these stones to raise up children to Abraham." (Lk. 3:8)

Mary is "full of grace" because of her faith, humility, and obedience, not because God gave her unfair preferential treatment. So, it is important not to misinterpret Mark 5:35 as contradicting Luke which says Mary is "full of grace" and "blessed among all women," and the "henceforth all generations" will call her blessed.

When Jesus dwells in us through faith, and the sacraments, we have the same mother and father as He does. We are sons and daughters of God as scriptures say, "he gave power *to become children of God;* {13} who were born, not of blood nor of the will of the flesh nor of the will of man, but of God." (Jn. 1:12,13) To deny the role of Mary as our mother in the family of God is to deny the full force of scripture and tradition from the earliest times in the Church.

As little children, God gave us our human parents to be the ones that first show us his love. They represent God to us when we are little, and then they teach us to love God as we grow. God loves us through them, and we love God through them. He commands us, "Honor your father and mother" (this is the first commandment with a promise), {3} "that it may be well with you and that you may live long on the earth." (Eph. 6:3) It is the only commandment with a promise or blessing attached to it. Why is this? It is because we owe them so much. They give their lives for us, and the God of justice expects us to return that love and honor to them. So it is with the spiritual family of God which we enter through Holy Baptism. When we honor the saints because they love God we honor and love God. The saints were given to us by God to help us love him and one another.

God the Father is the head of the family of God, and so he receives the highest honor, which is worship. But God has placed us in a family, and calls us to honor the other members as well. And he does the same, for he honors those who honor him. Jesus praised John the Baptist as the greatest prophet, and the scriptures are written to inspire us by the lives of faithful followers of God. The sacred stories of scripture help us to love God. And, so God expects us in turn to honor them for their love of God and man, as he honors them for their love of God and man. They are our elder brothers and sisters in the family of God, they are examples of love for us to help us, and people in our family in heaven who also help us by their prayers. The family of God extends between heaven and earth. When we honor them it pleases God, and helps us love God and our neighbor. We are called to be part of the family of God, to be one of the saints. When we are in the family of God, the saints are our siblings. Among the saints, there is the highest saint, Mary. She is the Queen of angels and saints. So, she is worthy of an even higher honor than the other saints. She has a special role at the right side of her son, for she is the Queen Mother in the kingdom of God and the family of saints.

Do not be Jealous of Mary, but Imitate Mary and Be Blessed

"Blessed rather are those who hear the word of God and keep it!" (Lk. 11:27, 28)

How did Jesus teach us not to be jealous of Mary's great holiness and honor as His Mother? By pointing out that Mary's holiness and ours consist in obedience to God's word, not in a physical relationship to Christ. The Pharisees were notorious for using their physical relationship as descendants of Abraham, instead of their own obedience to God, as their means to justification. (See Mt. 3, Jn. 8) Jesus saw the error of the woman in the crowd and stopped this kind of thinking immediately. This woman in the crowd is being gently spiritually chastised by Jesus. She is clearly redirected in her thinking to raise her sights from the physical, to what they should be on—the spiritual. The passage in question reads:

"As he said this, a woman in the crowd raised her voice and said to him, "Blessed is the womb that bore you, and the breasts that you sucked!" But he said, "Blessed rather are those who hear the word of God and keep it!" (Lk. 11:27, 28)

Mary **is** the one who heard the word of God and kept it or obeyed it. Some misunderstand this passage as denying honor to Mary, this is a great misunderstanding of the words of Jesus. He does not deny her blessedness as His Mother, which the same gospel teaches earlier *"Blessed are you among women."* (Lk. 1:42) Rather, he points to what made her blessed. Jesus does not teach in contradiction to the Holy Spirit, there can be no contradiction between Luke 1:42 and Luke 11:27, 28. The woman does not say the same words that The Holy Spirit says through Elizabeth. They have similar words, but the phrase has a different meaning. The words of the Holy Spirit bless Mary as a person, not her body parts. Notice the difference in the words:

Luke 1:42: Blessed are *you* among women, and blessed is the *fruit* of your womb.

Luke 11:27 Blessed is the *womb* that bore you, and the *breasts* that you sucked!

In Luke 1:42 we see the Holy Spirit inspiring Elizabeth to proclaim Mary is blessed among women, thus blessing her person. Then we see Elizabeth blessing Jesus, the fruit of her womb, thus blessing His person. The Holy Spirit says *"Blessed are you among women"* blessing the person of Mary, not her reproductive organ or nursing organ, and *"blessed is the fruit of your womb"* which is Jesus. This second blessing is blessing Jesus, and the word "womb" is mentioned in Luke 1:42 as in Luke 11:27, but the meaning is totally different. The womb is mentioned as a connection to Mary's role as Jesus' mother, but the honor or blessing of the verse isn't the "womb" it is Jesus who is the *"fruit of your womb."*

In Luke 11:27 the blessing is directed toward the function of Mary's body through birth and nursing. It is clear from the difference in the object being blessed, that the intention is different between the woman in the crowd in Luke 11 and the Holy Spirit speaking through Elizabeth in Luke 1. The woman in the crowd is envious of Mary's role as His mother. She is discouraged because she has not been chosen for this great blessing. The woman is seeing blessedness in being His mother, whereas Jesus points out Mary's blessing was not primarily a result of being His physical mother. Mary's blessing was primarily through obedience to God's commandments, a blessing available to us all. This is so that we do not become jealous or discouraged by her great honor as His Mother.

Mary: Queen of the Chessboard
of Heaven and Earth

"In your majesty ride forth victoriously for the cause of truth and to defend the right; let your right hand teach your dread deeds! {5} Your arrows are sharp in the heart of the king's enemies; the peoples fall under you. {6} Your divine throne endures for ever and ever. At your right hand stands the queen in gold of Ophir. With joy and gladness they are led along as they enter the palace of the king." (Psalm 45)

Our Lord taught using analogies or parables all the time. He did this to use concrete things to help us better understand spiritual realities. Do I dare compare Mary the Queen of Heaven and Earth to a queen on a chessboard? Yes, I do compare with an analogy for the purpose of teaching and understanding. And, I do so with a clean conscience because an analogy means there are some similarities, but differences remain. So, an analogy does not mean that the things compared are equal, and I would certainly never say a queen on a chessboard was equal to Our Lady the Queen of Heaven. St. Teresa of Avila is a Doctor of the Church and the Patroness of Chess players, who obviously knew how to play chess. She makes her own analogy of chess with the spiritual life in her book the Way of Perfection. She compares Christ to the king on the chessboard for the purpose of teaching us about spirituality. She writes:

"I hope you do not think I have written too much about this already; for I have only been placing the board, as they say. You have asked me to tell you about the first steps in prayer; although God did not lead me by them, my daughters I know no others, and even now I can hardly have acquired these elementary virtues. But you may be sure that anyone who cannot set out the pieces in a game of chess will never be able to play well, and, if he does not know how to give check, he will not be able to bring about a checkmate. Now you will reprove me for talking about games, as we do not play them in this house and are forbidden to do so. That will show you what kind of a mother God has given you—she even knows about vanities like this! However, they say that the game is sometimes legitimate. How legitimate it will be for us to play it in this way, and, if we play it frequently, how quickly we shall give checkmate to this Divine King! He will not be able to move out of our check nor will He desire to do so.

"It is the queen which gives the king most trouble in this game and all the other pieces support her. There is no queen who can beat this King as well as humility can; for humility brought Him down from Heaven into the Virgin's womb and with humility we can draw Him into our souls by a single hair. Be sure that He will give most humility to him who has most already and least to him who has least. I cannot understand how humility exists, or can exist, without love, or love without humility, and it is impossible for these two virtues to exist save where there is great detachment from all created things.

"You will ask, my daughters, why I am talking to you about virtues when you have more than enough books to teach you about them and when you want me to tell you only about contemplation. My reply is that, if you had asked me about meditation, I could have talked to you about it, and advised you all to practice it, even if you do not possess the virtues. For this is the first step to be taken towards the acquisition of the virtues and the very life of all Christians depends upon their beginning it. No one, however lost a soul he may be, should neglect so great a blessing if God inspires him to make use of it. All this I have already written elsewhere, and so have many others who know what they are writing about, which I certainly do not: God knows that.

"But contemplation, daughters, is another matter. This is an error which we all make: if a person gets so far as to spend a short time each day in thinking about his sins, as he is bound to do if he is a Christian in anything more than name, people at once call him a great contemplative; and then they expect him to have the rare virtues which a great contemplative is bound to possess; he may even think he has them himself, but he will be quite wrong. In his early stages he did not even know how to set out the chess board, and thought that, in order to give checkmate, it would be enough to be able to recognize the pieces. But that is impossible, for this King does not allow Himself to be taken except by one who surrenders wholly to Him." (St. Teresa of Avila, *The Way of Perfection*)

Although St. Teresa uses her analogy of the chess board to teach about the virtue of humility, I use my chess analogy to teach about the value of devotion to Mary. As we make our next move on the chessboard of life, we move across squares of darkness and light, places where we are threatened, and places where we are safe. Sometimes the dark knight of satan will seek to attack us, and sometimes the white knights of angels and saints will help protect us. Our guardian angel is like a white knight that protects us. We seek to protect our King from capture. Some may say how can you compare the king on the chessboard with Christ the King? Well as I said before an analogy shows similarities for teaching purposes. Our very existence depends upon the continuing permission of Christ so there is of course no comparison on this level. However we may still find some interesting things to compare with the chessboard and the spiritual life. On the chessboard we seek to protect the King. In this sense we seek to protect the presence of Christ the King within our souls. So when we commit a mortal sin, the presence of sanctifying grace, the presence of Christ the King within our souls, is lost. St. Paul speaks of this:

"Examine yourselves, to see whether you are holding to your faith. Test yourselves. Do you not realize that Jesus Christ is in you?—unless indeed you fail to meet the test! {6} I hope you will find out that we have not failed." (2Cor. 13:5, 6)

The Queen is the most powerful piece on the board; she is worth more than the pawn, the knight, the rook, or the bishop. However, the King is the most valuable piece on the board. This is where the analogy weakens between a king on a chessboard and the King of heaven. In the real world all of our power comes from Christ, and he cannot lose against his opponents. However, *we* can lose and we do so when we lose him! This is not the defeat of a chess game, but of our eternal soul. To die in mortal sin is the eternal checkmate of our soul! Conversely, to die in a state of grace is the final victory for our soul and a checkmate to our opponent. So, in our efforts for final victory we ask for the prayers of the Queen of Heaven: "pray for us sinners, now and at the hour of our death"!

For the sake of our spiritual chess analogy we consider the King as a symbol for Christ, the Queen as a symbol for Mary, the Bishop as a symbol for the priesthood and the sacraments, the Knight as a symbol for the angels—especially our guardian angel, the castle as a symbol for the Church and its teachings, and the pawns are a symbol for the average Christian. So, don't the pawns, rejoice when the Queen comes to protect them from the attacks of the enemy forces? So, on the chessboard the Queen comes to protect the less powerful pieces, and they are in a sense comforted by her presence. Through the daily Rosary we are comforted and protected by her presence. The King is the most important piece on the board, for if we lose him we lose the game. We can still win at chess without the queen, but it is much more difficult. The Queen brings a powerful protection for she is the mightiest piece on the board. Mary is the mightiest of all the saints, and she helps us lesser saints to be protected from temptations to sin so we do not lose our souls. Just as the chess player is comforted by having his queen still on the board, so too is the Christian who has the prayers of Mary in the Rosary comforted by having the Queen of heaven still with him in his fight. For, he fights to protect the presence of Christ within his soul from the checkmate of mortal sin. True we can re-enter the game of salvation when we repent of a mortal sin and are cleansed by confession; however, after any sin our position is changed on the board of life and salvation. We must proceed with greater zeal and do penances, to prove all the more our love for Christ, just as a player who loses one of his pieces must play harder to still win.

Trying to win the spiritual battle without the help of Mary's prayers is like trying to win a chess game without the queen. It is much more difficult to do without the help of the queen. So, maybe the next time you look at a queen on a chessboard, you might see her as a faint symbol of Mary, and remember your Queen in heaven who loves you with the love of a mother. For the Queen of heaven waits for you to pray the Rosary that she may comfort and protect you on the spiritual battlefield. The importance and dangers of the spiritual battlefield far exceed the size and dangers of the 64 squares of the chess battlefield. In the small pieces of the game of chess we see a hint of the power of a king and a queen in reality. In the spiritual battlefield we must remember that Christ is the King of Kings, and Mary is the Queen of Queens. They are our greatest allies in the battle of salvation. The absence of their presence adversely affects our position on the board of life, but their presence together is an eternally royal and winning combination. The eternal majesty of the King and Queen of heaven is a wonderful thing for us and a great terror to our enemy. Our Lady is the Queen of the chessboard of heaven and earth, let us move toward her and be kept safe.

"Who is this that looks forth like the dawn, *fair as the moon, bright as the sun, terrible as an army with banners?* How graceful are your feet in sandals, *O queenly maiden!*" (Song of Songs 6:10, 7:1)

The Immaculate Heart of Mary: The Flame, The Flower and the Sword

"...and a sword will pierce through your heart..." (Lk. 2:35)

The traditional image of the Immaculate Heart of Mary shows a flame, which symbolizes her love of God as it does with other servants:

"Of the angels he says, 'Who makes his angels winds, and his servants flames of fire.'" (Heb. 1:7)

The image of her heart also shows a flower, which symbolizes her purity from sin as scripture says:

"I am a rose of Sharon, a lily of the valleys."(Song of Songs 2:1)

100

Finally, there is a sword which symbolizes her sorrow over the effects of sin—especially the crucifixion of her only beloved son. St. Luke is the first to mention the heart of Mary in the scripture:

"But Mary kept all these things, pondering them in her heart." (Lk. 2:19)

The Miraculous Medal, the Green Scapular, and Our Lady of Fatima all contributed to a greater understanding of the importance of the Immaculate Heart of Mary. The Miraculous Medal was given to St. Catherine Laboure, a Daughter of Charity, on November 27, 1830. On front of the image was the prayer:

"O Mary conceived without sin, pray for us who have recourse to thee."

On the back of the medal was the depiction of the Sacred Heart of Jesus and the Immaculate Heart of Mary. The Sacred Heart of Jesus was encircled by a crown of thorns, symbolizing His passion, topped with a flame, symbolizing his love for men. The Immaculate Heart of Mary is pierced by a sword, symbolizing the agony of sorrow she felt at the foot of the cross. Michaelangelo's Pietà starts to capture this sorrow artistically, and gives us some insight. The silent suffering and sorrow of Mary is probably the greatest of all the saints, yet this is something few consider. Although Mary was not physically a martyr, her sinlessness caused her to suffer in sorrow far greater than we who are sinners. Her suffering and sorrow is so great scripture prophesies it. The sword through her heart is not just an artistic symbol, it was for her a painful reality. St. Simeon prophesied this in scripture:

"...and a sword will pierce through your own [heart] soul also, that thoughts out of many hearts may be revealed...and his mother kept all these things in her heart." (Lk. 2:35, 51)

Mary promised that great graces would be given to those who wore the medal. It has become known as the "Miraculous Medal" because of the many miraculous spiritual healings or conversions it has brought. It has also become known for physical healing and protection. I have a great devotion to the Miraculous Medal. This medal, which was given to me by my father when I was 14, was instrumental in my coming to grow in my faith in Christ, and devotion to the Rosary.

The Green Scapular was given in an apparition to Sister Justine Bisqueyburo, Daughter of Charity, in Paris, France. On September 8, 1840, the Feast of the Nativity of Mary, she appeared to the sister holding her Immaculate Heart, surrounded by flames, pierced with a sword, and topped by a golden cross. The vision of her heart was encircled with an inscription that read:

"Immaculate Heart of Mary, pray for us now, and at the hour of our death."

In her hand Mary had a scapular which would be known as the "Badge of the Immaculate Heart of Mary." Those who kept the green scapular on their person and prayed the prayer have received physical health, spiritual peace of mind and conversion.

In the apparition at Fátima, Portugal, 1917, Our Lady said:

"My Immaculate Heart will be your refuge and the way that will lead you to God... Sacrifice yourselves for sinners and say many times, especially whenever you make some sacrifice: 'O Jesus, it is for love of You, for the conversion of sinners, and in reparation for the sins committed against the Immaculate Heart of Mary... [the children were granted a vision of hell which frightened them very much.] You have seen Hell where the souls of poor sinners go. To save them, **God wishes to establish in the world devotion to My Immaculate Heart.** If what I say to you is done, many souls will be saved and there will be peace. The war is going to end; if people do not cease offending God, a worse one will break out during the pontificate of Pius XI. When you see a night illumined by an unknown light, know that this is the great sign given you by God that He is about to punish the world for its crimes, by means of war, famine, and persecutions of the Church and of the Holy Father. To prevent this, I shall come to ask for the consecration of Russia to My Immaculate Heart, and the Communion of Reparation on the First Saturdays. If My requests are heeded, Russia will be converted, and there will be peace; if not, she will spread her errors throughout the world, causing wars and persecutions of the Church. The good will be martyred, the Holy Father will have much to suffer, various nations will be annihilated. In the end, My Immaculate Heart will triumph. The Holy Father will consecrate Russia to Me, and she

will be converted, and a period of peace will be granted to the world. In Portugal the dogma of the Faith will always be preserved... When you pray the Rosary, say after each mystery: 'O my Jesus, forgive us, save us from the fire of Hell. Lead all souls to heaven, especially those who are most in need.'" (Words of Our Lady of Fatima, given to Lucia.)

After those in scripture, the earliest references of devotion to the Immaculate Heart of Mary are given by St. John Eudes. He composed Masses and offices in honor of the Hearts of Jesus and Mary. He celebrated the first feast of the Holy Heart of Mary on February 8, 1648. The apparition of the Miraculous Medal moved this devotion further into the hearts of the faithful in 1830. Eventually, the feast of the Immaculate Heart of Mary was instituted by Pope Pius XII in 1944 to be celebrated on August 22. In 1969, Pope Paul VI moved the celebration of the Immaculate Heart of Mary to Saturday after the Solemnity of the Sacred Heart of Jesus.

In view of the many references to the Immaculate Heart of Mary by the Popes, the Saints, the Marian Apparitions of the Miraculous Medal and Fatima, I believe it deserves to be raised to a Solemnity. It is my hope that the feast of the Immaculate Heart of Mary will one day be united to the Solemnity of the Sacred Heart of Jesus. It could be called: "The Solemnity of the Sacred Heart of Jesus and the Immaculate Heart of Mary."

The Hearts of Jesus and Mary are next to each other on the back of the Miraculous Medal, and Our Lady of Fatima showed that it was God's wish for the Sacred Heart and Immaculate Heart to be honored together. In the prayer of consecration to Mary called "Immaculata," written by saint and martyr, Maximillian Kolbe, we find the two hearts mentioned:

"O Immaculata, Queen of Heaven and earth, refuge of sinners and our most loving Mother, God has willed to entrust the entire order of mercy to you. I, (name), a repentant sinner, cast myself at your feet, humbly imploring you to take me with all that I am and have, wholly to yourself as your possession and property. Please make of me, of all my powers of soul and body, of my whole life, death and eternity, whatever most pleases you.

"If it pleases you, use all that I am and have without reserve, wholly to accomplish what was said of you: 'She will crush your head,' and 'You alone have destroyed all heresies in the whole world.' Let me be a fit instrument in your immaculate and merciful hands for introducing and increasing your glory to the maximum in all the many strayed and indifferent souls, and thus help extend as far as possible the blessed kingdom of the most Sacred Heart of Jesus. For wherever you enter you obtain the grace of conversion and growth in holiness, since it is through your hands that all graces come to us from the most Sacred Heart of Jesus.

V. Allow me to praise you, O Sacred Virgin
R. Give me strength against your enemies. Amen."

Pope Pius XII encouraged the joint devotion to the hearts in the 1956 encyclical *Haurietis Aquas*. He wrote:
"In order that favors in great abundance may flow on all Christians, nay, on the whole human race, from the devotion to the most Sacred Heart of Jesus, let the faithful see to it that to this devotion the Immaculate Heart of the Mother of God is closely joined." (*Haurietis Aquas.*)
Pope *John Paul II* explained the theme of unity of Mary's Immaculate Heart with the Sacred Heart in the 1979 encyclical *Redemptor Hominis*. He wrote:
"We can say that the mystery of the Redemption took shape beneath the heart of the Virgin of Nazareth when she pronounced her "fiat." From then on, under the special influence of the Holy Spirit, this heart, the heart of both a virgin and a mother, has always followed the work of her Son and has gone out to all those whom Christ has embraced and continues to embrace with inexhaustible love." (*Redemptor Hominis*)
On September 15, 1985 Pope John Paul II spoke of *The Alliance of the Hearts of Jesus and Mary* in his Angelus address. He addressed this "alliance" as his topic to the international conference at Fátima, Portugal in 1986. Loving Jesus with the heart of Mary was a theme

given by Pope John Paul II, and it shows how the love of the Immaculate Heart of Mary leads us to grow faster in the love of the Sacred Heart of Jesus.

In writing on the Rosary Pope John Paul II said:

"With the Rosary, the Christian people sit at the school of Mary and is led to contemplate the beauty of the face of Christ and to experience the depths of his love...Against the background of the words Ave Maria the principal events of the life of Jesus Christ pass before the eyes of the soul....and they put us in living communion with Jesus through—we might say—*the heart of his Mother.*" (*Rosarium Virginis Mariae*)

At Fatima Our Lady asked for the consecration of Russia to her Immaculate Heart. Consecration to the Hearts of Jesus and Mary is becoming a great tradition in the lives of the Saints. I believe it is important for us all to be consecrated to the Sacred Heart of Jesus and the Immaculate Heart of Mary. I often ask parents to consecrate their children to the Sacred Heart of Jesus and the Immaculate Heart of Mary after the rite of Baptism. It is my hope that one day a consecration would be included at the end of the official rite of Baptism. Pope Pius XII says:

"Consecration to the Mother of God, is a total gift of self, for the whole of life and for all eternity; and a gift which is not a mere formality or sentimentality, but effectual, comprising the full intensity of the Christian life—Marian life. This consecration tends essentially to union with Jesus, under the guidance of Mary." (Pope Pius XII)

I wrote this short prayer of combined consecrations many years ago:

The Consecration Prayer

I consecrate myself, all my thoughts, words, and actions, to the Most Holy Trinity, The Father, Son, and Holy Spirit—the Creator, the Redeemer, and the Sanctifier.

I consecrate myself to the Most Sacred Heart of Jesus, the Savior of the world, the Son of God, and the Son of man.

I consecrate myself to the Immaculate Heart of Mary, Queen of the Most Holy Rosary, the Mother of God, and the Mother of Mankind. Amen.

Other Titles by Fr. Herbert Burke:

A Scriptural Catechism

A Scriptural Catechism
Expanded Edition (English or Spanish)

The Rosary is the Answer

The Seven Fountains of Grace
A Scriptural Guide to the Sacraments

A Scriptural Guide to the Saints

A Scriptural Guide to the Priesthood